MW00633218

LOVE UP YOUR LIFE
BY AMIRAH HALL

What people are saying about this book...

"Save yourself from headaches, disappointments, and money down the drain. Read !...before you spend another night wishing things were different in your life. Amirah puts you on the fastest track to relationship success."

Suzanne, Cardiff, CA

"It's so great to be able access your natural attractiveness and sexiness. This book is inspiring and simple. Now that's an unbeatable combination. The visualizations are easy and Amirah offers encouraging tips to get you back into action. Now it's time to start turning heads."

Richard, Chicago, IL.

"This is not a book on how to love. It is a book on how to get the love in your life flowing. It is full of the shortcuts and how-to's, experiences only an insider could know. Whether you are working on an existing relationship or want to create one, you will find Amirah's wisdom and guidance invaluable.

Jane, La Jolla, CA

"Excellent book! I am so grateful to Amirah for sharing these powerful visualizations. I have spring in my step and feel myself coming out of my shell. In only two weeks I am getting so much male attention I can't believe it! Strangers have expressed they sense something about me. It really is as 'magical' as Amirah says."

Kelly, San Diego, CA

"I feel stronger and better about getting attention from the opposite sex. After working with the visualizations a couple of times, I ran into my old boyfriend. We hadn't seen each other in two years and have fallen in love all over again."

Jennifer, La Mesa, CA

"The work is powerful! After doing the visualizations only 5 times, I feel awake and alive like never before. Men are approaching me like never before. The results are immediate. I'm not used to this amount of positive attention – I love it!"

Laurie, Scottsdale, AZ

Table of Contents

Forward

H it's Amirah from www.amirahhall.com If you are asking, "how can I get a vibrant, juicy and jazzed up life that you love?" then this book is for you. This book guides you in revitalizing your energy vibes so that you begin shifting how you feel about yourself and the world around you. This gentle process acts like a love magnet attracting desirable loving experiences into your life.

You might be at a place in your life where you aren't feeling attractive ... or getting the love you feel you deserve. Has your current relationship lost its sizzle? You might be feeling as though your sexual desire has waned. Then again, you may not even have a sex life happening right now... Maybe you just want to feel alive and passionate about living. Regardless if you are on a mission to get on a fast track to marriage or looking for some spring in your stp...LOVE UP Your life will jump start you into blossoming love vibes.

Most people are unaware of what and how they are creating their current situations, or how to change it. The working dynamics of loving and healthy sexual relationships are for many people one of the greatest mysteries of life. It is a secret many of us seek to unravel. Others have simply given in to be alone. But you don't have to.

Your current situation is a result of your current energetic vibration. If you were hurt in the past, you may have shut down your sexual energy center. Beyond your conscious awareness; your energetic baggage is wrapped up neatly within the vibes you put out to the world. Even if you think you let go of past experiences, their energetic scars are still with you. Until you release energetic scars, or old thoughts and beliefs, you continue to attract more of the same. To have more love and attract what you truly desire in your life, you must change your energetic vibration.

Where are you now in your relationships? Do you want to increase your sex appeal? Are you ready to feel more attractive or loving? Are you discouraged about not getting what you want? For many people having the love they want and feeling attractive can sometimes feel unattainable.

Releasing energetic blocks that impede your natural attractiveness is KEY. As you begin to feel better about yourself, people will begin to notice you differently. Improve your self-esteem and confidence level, and that increases your libido. Undo past programming allows you access pleasure centers that have been closed down. You can become a sex magnet. Eliminate selflimiting beliefs, emotions and hidden programming and attract positive experiences. When you feel loving, you will attract more love.

When you feel good about yourself, you attract others to you. As you restore your natural vibrant attractiveness and love energy, you incorporate positive, loving feelings into your life. Then, you reveal your innate power and beauty within and attract the type of relationships you truly desire. It's magical! It works! It's powerful!

www.amirahhall.com © 2015
LOVE UP Your Life   amirah@amirahhall.com

In private consultations, clients continually ask author, Amirah Hall about finding and/or keeping Mr./Ms. Wonderful". She responded by creating this simple, step-by-step road map into the world of love and attraction. A seasoned professional who has walked the walk, Amirah personally practices the steps outlined in this book and knows first hand how it works.

With practice, this process is fast, effective and promises immediate results. Be open and receptive to possibilities. Discover the necessary elements to make your personal dreams real. Get frisky, flirty and most of all – have FUN!

Let me guide you! I have been professionally mentoring and enriching people just like you for over 15 years. Begin accessing and balancing your own unique energy vibes. Revealing your innate beauty and power within is the ultimate attraction secret to having the type of relationships you desire.

Step into a world of loving and self-healing YOU with - LOVE UP Your Life.

You've been waiting too long. Read on and apply all the simple steps, listen to the guided meditations and create a more loving and attractive you!

LISTEN to LOVE UP Your Life Guided Meditation

http://amirahhall.com/images/audio/loveupyourlife.mp3

www.amirahhall.com © 2015
LOVE UP Your Life

amirah@amirahhall.com

CHAPTER ONE

Get Grounded to Attract More Love

a re you at a place in your life where you aren't attracting the love you want?

Has your current relationship lost its sizzle? In this chapter, you will learn about grounding and how it helps overcome resistance to having the love you desire. As you begin to feel better about yourself, people will begin to notice you differently.

Grounding Defined

IF YOU HAVE ever been light-headed from hunger and then felt a sigh of contentment as you fed your body the perfect meal, you've experienced grounding. If you've ever melted into the back rub you got from a trusted person at the end of a stressful day, you've experienced being grounded. Grounding is a simple process of connecting to the Earth that many people do naturally throughout the course of a day. Anything that brings you to the sense of pleasure and release is grounding. When you are grounded, you feel centered focused, and present.

People connect with their bodies and the Earth in many ways: through touch and body work, through eating, through being out in nature or in water, through contact with animals and through healthy sex. Visualizing, an imaginary grounding cord, is a way to release foreign energy from your body so that it can experience love and joy.

Create a Path for Releasing to Feel Safe and Happy

A GROUNDING CORD provides a way to flush out pent up energy and emotion so you can feel good about yourself. It is a way to move energy as it comes towards you, rather than letting it get stuck in the body. When foreign energy gets stuck in the body, it stops the natural flow of energy and might manifest as depression, a migraine headache, aches, pain, or eventually illness.

A former client, Kim, developed a mind-bending migraine headache while at Knott's Berry Farm with her family. At one point, the migraine got the best of her and she was forced to sit out a ride. She found a quiet spot away from the amusement park mania and sat down. She visualized a grounding cord from the base of her spine to the center of the planet. Then, she hooked the imaginary cord to the center of the planet. Giving her permission to start releasing all foreign energy, her body began to relax. Within ten minutes, Kim experienced a tremendous relief as the pain slowly dissipated and was thrilled the technique worked. She was elated to be able to heal herself in a chaotic amusement park and is confident she can take this tool with her any place. Her husband and kids were happy too because their fun didn't have to stop.

For More Love and Joy Release What You Don't Want

IN ORDER TO make room for what you do want, you have to release and let go of the things you don't want. To attract what you want, you will want to let go of everything that keeps you away from Love. Like attracts like.

Unless you want to continue on your current path, you are probably overdue to let go of emotional pain of a break-up or the need for approval. Maybe you continuously seek recognition at work or have unrealistic expectations for yourself. Thoughts like, "I'm not attractive" or "I will never have a loving relationship" need to be purged. You will begin to attract what you desire as you let go of doubts, negative self-talk, apathy and rejection. All activities, including conversations can be cleared from your space daily to give you more room for joyful expression.

Kathy attended a recent workshop because her friend thought she would benefit from learning the techniques in this book. She went through a painful and traumatic divorce over ten years ago and she has not had sex or been on a single date since. She was looking for hope that she might overcome her fears about dating and having sex. The thought of going on a date, she thought, would be an actual miracle. To her surprise two weeks later, after one workshop session, Kathy went on her first date in ten years. In letting go of restrictions, fear and insecurity she created hope for romance in her life. With each passing day, she feels more confident and enthusiastic about potential love interests.

www.amirahhall.com © 2015   amirah@amirahhall.com
LOVE UP Your Life

Flush-Out Pent-Up Energy to Get the Lovin' Feelin'

LIFE SEEMS TO just flow more easily and the body uses less energy when it is grounded. Grounding allows us to overcome resistance and connect with the physical body. In our society, people have lost touch with the reality of their body. Our lives are busy from dawn to dusk. We are on the verge of sensory overload.

Grounding is a simple and a powerful way to intuitively connect with your self and stay connected with the stabilizing nature of Earth energy. You will get things on your To-Do List accomplished with less time, more effectively. As you flush out the stresses of the day, or tension from the work week, you have more energy to create that 'lovin' feelin'.

Attract Others to You Without Trying

DO YOU KNOW anyone unfocused, forgetful, overwhelmed, or heavily invested in controlling everything around them? They may forget conversations, over commit themselves to others, waste endless time searching for keys, or miss their freeway exit.

Maybe you feel frustrated, unsettled, or challenged to be around people like that. Ungrounded people are in pain - emotional, mental, or physical. When you use your grounding cord to release pain, old beliefs, programs, discomfort, resentment, expectations you will begin to notice how easily you attract without effort.

On the other hand, naturally grounded people are generally pleasant, centered, and focused. It feels safe to be around them. They solve problems easily and life appears to flow effortlessly for them. Their communications are clear, they recall details easily, and are organized. Their sustained energy levels help them attract affection from others and romance in their life.

It feels good to be around a grounded person. Grounded people are more attractive. You may have even heard yourself say, "He/she is so grounded! I'd like to be like him/her." Can you see yourself walking up to someone new, smiling and radiating confidence?

One client came to me because he was frustrated with his grounding practice. During his practice, Andy imagined his grounding cord but it seemed to stop before it reached the center of the earth. He was not grounded. With practice, he began to feel more solid and centered.

Grounding is such an invaluable tool in healing yourself that it's worth taking the time to be sure you can do it easily and comfortably. With practice, you can train yourself to be connected with the earth all of the time.

Self-Love - Secret Tip #1

Create a new ritual for yourself. Start your day with a grounding cord. When you jump into the shower or brush your teeth create a new grounding cord for the new day. A perfect time to remind yourself to release is while you are in the restroom. Be amused with your release!

Effortless Release Every Day for More Harmony

GROUNDING WORKS MUCH like a drain or waterfall. When you pour water down the drain you probably never wonder ….:"where did it go?" Be patient with yourself and have fun with your new toy. Grounding becomes as natural as breathing or smiling with practice. Consider releasing other people's problems, your worries and anxiety that are weighing you down... Keep it simple and stay amused with yourself. Tune into being in harmony with this process of grounding and letting everything go effortlessly.

Remember

1. Start your day with grounding.

2. Check in with yourself during the day to see if you have a grounding cord.

3. Notice what happens in your body as you release using your grounding cord.

4. Practice a grounding meditation daily to activate your natural attractiveness.

Self Love - SECRET TIP #2

Practice the following grounding meditation 10-15 minutes each day.

You can always practice more. The more you practice, the better your results will be. Don't create any limits for yourself on how much you can release without effort.

---

www.amirahhall.com © 2015
LOVE UP Your Life

amirah@amirahhall.com

Create Harmony All Day - Anywhere or Anytime

GROUNDING HELPS MAKE your body feel safe. Notice if you have your grounding cord attached while standing in line at Starbucks, eating dinner or while at work. Ground yourself driving or playing sports. This will increase your focus and maybe even your game.

Kent, a scratch golfer and a former student of mine, began using his grounding cord while golfing and his score improved. His golf partners noticed his obvious improvement and were convinced he was secretly working with a new coach. That coach just happened to be me. His secret was his grounding cord. Use your grounding cord to better improve your balance, co-ordination and focus.

Your grounding cord can follow you wherever you go, whatever you do. Just imagine yourself connected to the earth, preventing foreign energy from sticking to your space.

> **Self-Love – SECRET TIP #3**
>
> **Create a post-it note for your fridge, bathroom mirror, or the back door to remind yourself to get grounded. Or try a pop-up reminder on your computer desktop. This way it will soon become part of your daily experience.**

Grounding Cord Visualization

TO REVITALIZE AND refresh your body, mind and spirit take the first step by letting go with grounding. It is always the first step to all the subsequent steps in this book. From the base of your spine, make a connection to the healing planet energy to release excess energy and stabilize your body. Follow along with the Grounding Guided Meditation - Quantum Energy Tool #1 https://www.youtube.com/watch?v=NBILZMUPKxQ

1. Close eyes but stay focused.

2. Be aware of your own body with your feet flat on the floor.

3. Create a mental image of a line of energy between base of spine and the center of the planet.

4. Connect a grounding cord into the center of earth.

5. Secure the grounding cord snuggly at the base of your spine.

6. Notice your breathing.

7. Using the gravitational pull of the planet start to release foreign or stuck energy from your body and aura.

8. Notice how your body feels while grounding. Imagine seeing stuck energy draining out of you.

Visualization Tip:

The center of the planet doesn't have to be 'fire and brimstone'. It might be a cool soothing lake. See your grounding cord as a waterfall or redwood tree. Let your imagination guide you

---

Now that you know about grounding and have practiced using your grounding cord, are you ready to use the natural rhythm of creating and destroying to be more loving?

www.amirahhall.com © 2015
LOVE UP Your Life

amirah@amirahhall.com

CHAPTER TWO

Use Natural Rhythms to Create and Attract

*H*ave you ever wished that you could create anything you want? And destroy the things that you don't want? Have you ever wished that you could wiggle your nose, and a pile of money would magically appear? Or, maybe make a wish upon a star, and it comes true?

Wishing upon a star may or may not work, but wishes can come true, hence the saying, "Be careful what you wish for." So, if wishes can come true, then just what is it that makes this happen? Wishes are just thoughts, right? Then there must be some sort of force, or energy in thoughts, that enables them to become things. In this chapter, you learn how to create and destroy to affect what you attract to yourself.

Everything is Basically Energy Even Thoughts and Feelings

LIKEWISE, YOUR MIND is composed of energy in a certain structural pattern. When your mind influences matter, in actual fact it is energy working upon itself in a certain way. Since energy is fluidic and kinetic in nature it flows where it is directed to by one's mental attention. The direction of energy is not limited by time or space. That is simply an illusion perceived by one's consciousness.

Most people lack the understanding of how the physical laws of creation work. Do you have fear, insecurity, anxiety, family programming or mental blocks that stop you from creating? Have you ever felt that you don't deserve to be loved? Are you putting off setting plans in motion because you might leave someone else behind? Do you think you are NOT worthy of having what you want?

Thought is the creator behind all operations of manifestations in the material world. These manifestations cannot occur until a suggestion, desire or thought, enters the Subconscious mind. The Subconscious mind then absorbs the thought, processes it and stores it.

Einstein once said,

"Thought is energy, to create it (energy), just use your imagination."

Learning how to harness that energy, and properly direct it into something solid is the process of creation. Everything starts with a thought. Your home was first a thought in the architect's mind. Your car started out in the mind of a designer or engineer. Everything that exists in the present moment was first a thought.

The reason so many of your thoughts fail to come into fruition in your life is that you judge them and discard them in your mind. Other thoughts that reached the emotional level were focused out or you don't feel a strong desire to make them happen. Over time, your mind becomes "blocked or programmed" with negativity from your surroundings and your ability to create is affected.

Creating Unconsciously

WHILE GROWING UP, parents, family, and friends bombard you with their thoughts, feelings, beliefs, habits and patterns. Likely, you absorbed some, if not most, of this programming. You stored it in your Subconscious mind and body. As time passes, storing this energy diminishes your own power to create. Are you unknowingly creating situations that you don't want? Do you wonder why you cannot attract what you want?

Destroying Your Creations

A GROUP OF Tibetan monks at the St. Louis Art Museum created a sand painting, where they meticulously position millions of grains of sand in a colorful pattern. After five days of work, they destroy their creation. The process serves as a way for the Buddhists to meditate, work to spread blessing, and show the temporary nature of ALL things in this world. Their practice symbolizes the impermanence of all existence and teaches the lesson of non-attachment. They believe it is important to NOT be too attached to the things of this world.

> *"To every thing there is a season, and a time to every purpose under the heaven: a time to be born, and a time to die; a time to plant, and a time to pluck up that which is planted; a time to kill, and a time to heal; a time to break down, and a time to build up . . . "*
>
> Ecclesiastes 13

Have you ever felt guilty when you release or destroy something, such as a relationship with a romantic partner, an agreement or commitment? Are you harboring old grudges, rejection or plans that never worked out? Is it difficult for you to let go of your old clothes or magazines?

When you consciously or unconsciously are unable to release thoughts from former relationships or past situations, they create blocks to what you want to create in your life. These blocks establish parameters that you create more of the same. You create continuously. Sometimes, you are so busy creating things that you don't allow time or space for new things you want to create.

When you clear out the fridge of moldy, forgotten leftovers, you create room for fresh groceries for delicious mouthwatering meals. After you tidy up the closet and send your discards to Goodwill, you make room for your fashion make-over.

You Create Your Reality

THE SIMPLEST WAY to put it is that the purpose of life is to learn to control energy. Learning to control your mental energy comes from using your thoughts and emotions to create the physical reality you desire. You then live successfully with the matter and events that are formed!

Learning to direct and focus your thoughts will reflect in changes in your physical world. The better your abilities at creating reality, the better you are able to learn, solve problems, create abundance, build joyful relationships, and help others.

When you visualize an object or symbol in your imagination, you are actually creating the object or symbol on an energetic level. This object or symbol has properties that can have an effect on the physical plane. When you imagine you are destroying the object or symbol, you are actually moving and changing the molecules that make up this energy form. When you create and destroy an object or symbol, an energy force is set in motion that affects all other energies surrounding it.

Therefore, you can use this process to move and release unwanted energies.

Many people have no inkling of their potential ability to create. People often say, "I don't have a creative bone in my body." These very people have jobs, children, houses, and bank accounts. Who created these things in their lives, if they didn't?

Is your judgment clouded? Do you feel you are living your life for other people and not yourself? Are you constantly plagued with anxiety and the fear that at any moment your life might change? Then you are resisting the vital flow of life itself; the natural rhythm of creating and destroying.

The Balance of Creating and Destroying

FROM BIRTH TO death, from preschool to high school graduation, from marriage to divorce, from beginning a new job to resigning from it, from purchasing a new dress to donating it to a used clothing store, from earning a nice fat paycheck to spending every penny of it, you are creating and destroying.

Your ability to create and destroy visualizations is directly related to the ability to create and destroy many other things in your life. When you create and destroy an object in your mind, you are moving energy and impacting everything around you.

Everyone Creates and Destroys Continuously

PEOPLE DIFFER DRASTICALLY in terms of their issues or beliefs surrounding creating and destroying. There are all kinds of emotions and thought forms that affect a person's ability to create or destroy.

Do you feel insecure about creating something different in your life? Do you feel blocked from even starting? Are you paralyzed by the thought of cleaning out your closet or letting go of old books?

Perception Creates Reality

THE WAY YOU perceive your present-day world is based on how your world has been in the past. The meanings you put on those experiences are based on that perception. There is no right or wrong in perception. Perception simply is! It can make whatever picture the mind desires.

If you perceive that creating a business is hard and risky, then, you are very right! Perhaps you had an experience like this before or sensed from others that it is hard and risky. If you perceivee that life is worthwhile, despite its many problems, then, you are also right! This will make you positive and confident everyday that all you manifest in your mind will come true.

Perception is made up of either illusion or reality. Illusion is defined as anything that is temporary in nature, that was thought up by man, and had a perception placed on it. When two or more people agree on this illusion, it then becomes reality.

A difference in perception has been the cause of many arguments, even war. The next time you encounter a difference in perception, rather than fight, ask yourself if you would rather be right or happy. What perceptions are blocking your ability to create the love you want in your life?

Are you ready to release their grip on a new perception of a present time reality?

Healing and Loving Yourself

THINK ABOUT WHAT you are creating if you are walking wounded. Is there something in your life you just can't seem to release - anger, hate, shock, or apparent failures? How can you feel successful when you go through life dead on the inside? How can you create a loving relationship or business when you focus on resentments and past pain? Even if you think a former relationship is behind you, some of its affect might be hidden unconsciously within you.

All illness has its primary origin in the mind rather than in the body. Stress and pain result from an imbalance somewhere in your being. Mental pain expresses itself in scattered thinking, mental blocks, limiting beliefs, and misperceptions.

Destroy Old Perceptions for Renewal

THE CONSCIOUS ALIGNING of your spiritual, mental and physical bodies brings you into a state of being that is totally healthful and rejuvenating. Having good physical, emotional and mental health gives your spirit a more powerful and energetic place to dwell. You can be more focused on your life's dreams, vision, and goals. Loving yourself will heal and change your life. You begin to heal yourself by recognizing your own worth, your true nature, without baggage.

When you lock-in on your belief, feeling or thought at that moment it becomes alive to you. This becomes part of what you are in the process of creating. It is the time to still all doubts and fears. Are you ready to lock-in new feelings, beliefs or thoughts that will become alive in you, creating a more loving vibe?

Create and Destroy Symbols to Heal

YOU DON'T HAVE to be consciously aware of all your blocks to clear them and create room for what you do want. Clear old thoughts and feelings from past experiences, disappointments, resentments to gain a new sense of freedom or lightness. Discharge emotions, resentments or other stagnant energy to restore your ability to manifest your dreams.

Blocked energy that has unconsciously shaped your experiences can be released without effort. This frees you to create a self-defined, authentic self that is grounded in the here and now.

Karen's former husband was an extremely controlling person who limited who she spoke with, where she went and how she dressed. When she divorced over ten years ago she thought she had reclaimed her freedom to live as she chose. What she wasn't aware of was that she was living in fear that no one would love her. Her husband's intimidation tactics left her feeling unconfident and resentful. This experience permeated every area of her life affecting her work, how she interacted with others and her thoughts of herself. Even though she made every effort to put it behind her, this energy unconsciously controlled her. With coaching, Karen began the practice of disintegrating the hidden programming and old beliefs to heal her self.

Decide which of your key external events has turned out to be the most toxic experience of your life. Then write a short description of the target event. When you're done, read it over to make sure you are being honest in your account. Then imagine depositing this experience into a symbol of a rose in your imagination and exploding the symbol. This exercise releases the blocked energy from the experience. This provides healing to your emotions and physical body and frees up space to create more of what you want.

Visualization Tip

Exploding your symbol might look like a bubble bursting, fireworks on the 4 of July, or an exploding firecracker. Be creative and let your imagination have fun.

Clearing Foreign Energy Visualization

TO RELEASE AND destroy blocks of energy, first create a grounding cord. Create a symbol in your mind's eye and fill it with what you want to release. Explode the symbol to release the energy from your space, healing yourself and returning the energy to it.

1. Imagine suspending a symbol 6" in front of you. A symbol might be a flower, a tree, a fence, a mirror, or a heart.

2. Allow this symbol to be an absorbing object.

3. Begin to allow this symbol to draw out and absorb any foreign energy, stuck thoughts, emotions or pictures from your body and the space around you.

4. Let the foreign energy appear as dark colors.

5. When the symbol is completely filled up with these dark colors, imagine exploding it into a billion pieces.

Self Love Tip #4

It's helpful to use the same type of object over a period of time so that you can intuitively notice if and when it changes. As it absorbs foreign energy your symbol may alter its appearance. Different situations may call for different sizes, strengths and qualities of symbols.

Do you want a more intimate and affectionate relationship with your spouse? Are you ready to attract more supportive friends to socialize or work with? Have you been neglecting your sexual needs and wishing for more stimulation?

www.amirahhall.com © 2015
LOVE UP Your Life
amirah@amirahhall.com

Some people make things happen. Others watch things happen. Then some people wonder what happened! Are you ready to consciously create a more loving and attractive reality so you can have more love in your life?

www.amirahhall.com © 2015
LOVE UP Your Life

amirah@amirahhall.com

CHAPTER THREE

Revitalize Your Love Vibe

The saying goes, love is in the air. But you may be thinking, "yea right!" Do you ever feel that you are invisible? Do you find yourself helping everyone else wondering when it's your turn to be loved? Is it hard to think and act for yourself? In this chapter learn how to revitalize your love vibes. Bit by bit, your ability to radiate and revitalize your love vibe will attract more desirable experiences. When you feel loving, you will attract more love. Feeling good about yourself, attracts others to you.

Replenish the Natural Loving You

IF YOU OBSERVE a wilted plant resurrect after it's watered, you have witnessed replenishing. If you ever experienced drinking a cold glass of water after being parched dry from thirst, then you experienced being replenished. Replenishing yourself is a simple process to reclaim your own vital energy from where you left it —with other people, places and situations.

> **FACT**
>
> Anything that brings you back to the place of feeling rejuvenated is replenishing to your spirit.

When you feel good about yourself, you are more likely to feel desirable and sexual. When you feel bad, you don't. When you feel loving, you effortlessly attract kindness and support. Replenishing yourself with your own vital reclaimed energy sweetens and changes old habituated negative patterns of mind. This is healing your troubled mind and spirit to free it from its pain and confusion.

Feel Motivated and Enthusiastic About Life and Love

YOUR SPIRIT IS powerful; it can go anywhere, anytime. It is not bound by your body. When you think of someone else or something else, your spirit or energy goes there. Part of your energy leaves your body and travels elsewhere. Imagine all the books you have ever read? Or all the gifts you gave? Or all the places you traveled to? You have left some of your energy on everything that you do or think about. Now, that's a sobering thought.

Often times your energy has been left in places like your work, projects you have been focused on, your spouse or partner's body or energy field, or even in your computer. Most people have large amounts of energy in the future or in the past.

When your energy goes into all of your relationships it makes it hard to focus on you and what you want to create. It becomes challenging to maintain balanced emotional, mental and physical health. When your energy is engaged in an unhappy or abusive relationship with a negative thinking or a mis-behaving person, you are vulnerable to illness and exhaustion. So much of your vital force goes into making things right that you become depleted.

Release Unwanted Thoughts

HAVE YOU EVER spent time thinking about past problems fearing they might happen again? When you think about your past problems, your energy goes into them. Have you spent time thinking ahead of yourself into the future preparing, planning or worrying about what is yet to come? When you jump into the past, future events or situations, it is difficult to appreciate and make the most of the present moment. What you think about; you bring about. When you spend time on unwanted thoughts or feelings it leaves less energy for you to just be.

Love Energy is Intoxicating

CAN YOU REMEMBER feeling in love? Love energy is intoxicating. Access that intoxicating love energy to incorporate positive, loving feelings into your life. Connecting to a loving feeling creates a feeling of safety and support. When you feel safe, you release anxiety, awkwardness and uneasiness, allowing your natural sexual expression to flow easily.

Self-Love Tip #5

Replace nervous energy with love energy.

Addicted to Your Job or Another Person?

ANYTIME SOMEONE SUFFERS from an addiction, whether to a substance, to their job, or to another person, they are experiencing a problem with their own energy flow. A dependency on anything or anyone, gives power to someone or something outside of you. You are basically giving all your energy to the addiction which feeds it further. One way to solve this problem is by using a technique to aid you in replenishing your own energy and self-energize.

Attachment is a By-Product of Love

WHEN YOU SEND loving feelings toward the person, spending time together, sharing experiences and activities, you become attached to them. Love is an expansive energy and enables you to grow into who you are. It's hard to relinquish the sense of security that develops from such closeness. This is why it often takes many messy attempts over time to fully let go of someone to whom you're attached.

If you constantly think of your lover, spouse, child, friend, or whoever, you are most likely giving them too much of your own vital energy, or their energy is occupying too much of your energetic field.

Restore Vibrant Attraction

EVEN IF YOU have a perfect relationship, when too much of your energy is directed in another relationship or person, you can become unbalanced. For example, you cannot use MAC software in a PC. Likewise, other people's energy doesn't work in your body. It's not about being good or bad – it just doesn't work for you. Your spirit contracted to have your body and it runs efficiently on your energy only!

Increase Your Vibrant Love Essence

RECLAIMING YOUR ENERGY will not only help stop unwanted thoughts, it will also decrease confusion and increase your ability to communicate with your own inner voice. To reclaim your own energy from people, places and situations, visualize a shimmering golden sun above your head. Allow it to magnetically reclaim your energy from places where you left it. Then, with your imagination, bring the golden sun down into your body, replenishing all the cells of your body. Imagine yourself engulfed with this powerful, vibrant essence of YOU.

The color of 'gold' is a vibration that is wonderful for healing since it is soothing, and neutralizes non-beneficial energy. Using the color gold as a cleansing and healing energy can shift your perspective, heal old wounds, help clarify situations, and generally help to get you in touch with your own spiritual perspective on life. It will also assist you to gently release old burdens from your body and open to creating new experiences. Gold is a favorite for many people; it is simple, amazingly powerful, and very accessible.

During your practice, try replenishing yourself using different colors. Allow them each to be your teacher and notice how or if you feel different with different colors. Some days or weeks you might feel an affinity with one color for no particular reason. Listen to your own inner guidance and experiment.

Revitalize Your Self – Any Time, Any Where

YOU CAN REPLENISH yourself all day long. While standing in a stagnant grocery line, after a grueling energy zapping meeting with your boss or during a soccer game with the kids, you can replenish your energy. Revitalize your drooping spirit any time during the day or while practicing the relaxing exercises in this book. You can 'ground' and 're-energize' yourself as often as desired. Begin to feel lighter, more alive, relaxed, and calm as you reclaim more of your energy. There is an infinite amount of energy you can reclaim into your space.

You Can Never Have Too Much Love!

A FACT OF life is that many people are troubled by difficult emotional states but do not develop the skills to deal with them. When your mind goes sour it is within your capacity to arouse positive feelings to sweeten it. Bring in as much replenishing energy as you can accept.

Experiment and add a touch of enthusiasm, clarity or confidence into the imaginary sun before giving it to yourself. When you feel good about yourself, you are more likely to feel sexual. When you feel bad, you don't feel sexual.

"People are about as happy as they make up their minds to be."

Abraham Lincoln 22

Self-Love Tip #6

Rather than begging your doctor for Viagra or ordering a dozen bottles of Passion ZX, give yourself more replenishing arousing energy. The long-term benefits will be so rewarding.

Abundance and Gratitude for Love

ON A DINNER date recently, my date and I wanted something rich and chocolaty to finish off our evening. The restaurant didn't have anything that appealed to our taste buds, so we decided to pass on dessert. Ten minutes later, our waiter surprised us with a decadent gourmet chocolate dessert on the house. Before this, I remember feeling content and abundant from the meal and appreciated the generosity of my date. I felt grateful for the entire evening. Feeling rich and grateful attracts generosity abundance.

Abundance is an aspect of perfection and is the natural state of the universe. We are always experiencing abundance. However, to have abundance in our lives requires a willingness to recognize that it is always available and we need only open ourselves to receive it.

Consider this, what you focus upon abundantly will grow. To achieve what you want, focus your attention on it if you focus abundantly on fear or impossibilities, you attract that to you. Imagine filling your golden suns with free gifts of affection, gratitude, patience and love to attract it abundantly into your life.

Lack of any kind in life is a direct message that you are failing to love yourself. Loving yourself will allow you to consciously direct tremendous abundance in your life. Gratitude is the key to directing abundant energy. Begin to consciously express gratitude for your world filled with abundant affection and love.

31

Replenish Yourself Visualization

TO EXPERIENCE THE abundance of love in your life, you must think and feel abundance all around you, by becoming aware, through conscious gratitude, moment by moment.

To replenish yourself, take the next step by attracting abundant love. Feel the sensation of the golden shimmering light embracing every cell of your body with love and attraction.

Close eyes but stay focused. Follow along with Replenishing Guided Meditation - Quantum Energy Tool #3 https://www.youtube.com/watch?v=CxuTq7uMnRc 1.

1. Be aware of own body with your feet flat on the floor.

2. Create a grounding cord from the base of your spine to the center of the planet.

3. Imagine a giant gold sphere or sun about 3 feet above your head.

4. Allow this sun to act like a powerful super-computer and retrieve your life force from wherever it is on the planet. It knows where you have been and where you want to go, what you've done, what you are thinking about. Everything you've done or thought of you left energy on it. Magnetically allow the sphere to collect your own energy.

5. Imagine your energy as bright colors coming back to the sphere. Observe the gold sphere getting bigger and brighter as your energy returns to it.

6. Allow the golden shimmering sphere to enter into your body through the crown chakra on the top of your head.

7. Picture the golden energy filling up every cell in your body, all the organs, tissue, body systems, blood, bones and aura, that energetic space that surrounds your body approximately two feet around you.

If you fall asleep or become unconscious while grounding or replenishing your energy, don't worry or become discouraged. This is

32

common in the beginning. If you drift off to sleep, bring your attention back to present time and pick up where you left off.

At times you might need to replenish with more of your own energy. You may need to bring in multiple gold spheres with your own energy. While practicing this technique, Adam got a sharp pain in the left leg. When he brought in several more golden suns into his body, the leg spasm released and he felt relaxed again. Never be afraid of giving yourself an abundance of your precious vibes.

Become What You Want

ENJOY FEELING RELAXED, calm, and still. You might feel like a GOLD MINE rich with treasure. This means you are present and recharging yourself. You are Healing. On the other hand, you may not feel anything. That's OK too. Everyone has their own experience. Be patient with yourself and the process. Be aware that whether you have a physical sensation or not, the technique is working. Practice grounding, creating and destroying and replenishing yourself to bring about positive attitudinal changes and systematically develop the quality of 'loving-attraction'.

When you have more of our own vital energy in your energetic space and body, you build momentum and attract more of what you desire. With practice, your energy becomes more powerful and magnetic. Without effort, you develop clarity and effortlessly become what you want. Your natural effervescence will begin to bubble up as you release accumulated stress and radiate your natural sensuality.

Incorporate your practice into your everyday life. Take your good vibes outside into the streets, at home, at work and into your relationships. Get ready to create more intimacy, attracting more attention that just might surprise you as you learn to re-sexualize your self.

> Love doesn't make the world go 'round. Love is what makes the ride worthwhile.
>
> Franklin P. Jones 25

CHAPTER FOUR

Re-Sexualize Your Self

*H*ave you ever wondered why you think about sex the way you do? Has someone told you that it was wrong to be sexual and dress sexy? Have you enjoyed a healthy, satisfying sex life most of your adulthood, but lately, intimate moments with your partner are less satisfying than they once were? Do you might feel as though your sexual desire has waned? Maybe you would just be happy to express your sexuality freely without feeling like a bimbo.

In this chapter, you will learn how to discharge thoughts and beliefs from past experiences to enhance your ability to express and attract love and affection.

Basic Sexual Instincts

THE CONDITIONING OF the body to be sexual and reproduce is the strongest on the planet. It is the second strongest instinct next to that of survival. Sexual desire is a normal and natural feeling for women and men. However, sexual desire can change over time, and can increase or decrease depending on the situation.

Do you worry about what is "normal" or "abnormal" sexual activity? Do you wonder why or what causes the change in your sex drive? Understandably every person, and every couple, has a different level of desire and need for sexual intimacy. In response to outside forces such as stress and emotional experiences, sexual desires often change.

Sexual Desire Versus Sexual Arousal

THERE'S A BIG difference between sexual desire and physical arousal. Your desire or libido refers to your interest in sex, while arousal refers to your body's physical response. Is your sex drive down? Do you have little interest in sex? Is it difficult for you to become aroused?

After attending a GET Better LOVE and MORE of IT workshop, Don was concerned because he noticed that since he practiced the Visualization exercises, his sex urge was stronger. After a few weeks, he detached from his obsessive sexual needs. When a person moves out any stuck thoughts and feelings, it creates space for balance and harmony within the body and mind.

Stored Energy From Your Past

DID YOU GET the message while growing up that sex is dirty? Or that your body must be hidden from view. Starting from the cradle, many people begin to ignore their bodies, and deny their potential for providing enjoyment.

The human body, from birth, is equipped with faculties: the five senses, the mind or sixth sense to interact with events and circumstances. These faculties are busy interpreting and reacting to events and circumstances giving rise to thoughts, actions and experiences. In everyday living, you unknowingly draw in large amounts of energy from your environment. You absorb this corrupt and foreign energy, condense and store it as memory.

This memory becomes the basis of physiological growth and is stored in the brain and every cell within the body. You absorb this foreign energy into your body, and over time, stack it layer upon layer, creating dense energetic blockages. With every passing year, these pockets of

amirah@amirahhall.com

energy expand, storing records of every experience, including feelings and thoughts relating to the experiences. So, when you realize this, you want to be sure to clear it out. If you want love in your life this stored energy must be refined.

Releasing Memories to Attract Love

SOME OF THESE stored pockets of energy stem from traumatic or emotionally charged experiences that act like a magnet for similar experiences and energies. Pockets of energy act as frames of reference that motivate and control your perceptions; they dictate the manner in which you interpret and react to every aspect of life.

As this energy accumulates in the physical body, the result can become weight gain, illness or dis-ease. Absorbed tension and foreign energy has a depressive or inhibiting affect on your natural attractive ability.

Perceptions Influence Your Love Ability

AS TIME PASSES, the energy from your collection of life experiences creates a snowball effect on how you react to people and situations. This energy has a strong influence on your perceptions, attitude and lifestyle. Over time you become more clouded, polluted, and your inner beauty dims from the accumulation of these foreign and stuck energies.

You are constantly bombarded by other people's thoughts. Your self-esteem is closely tied to how other people perceive you or how you think they perceive you, as well as the energy that they send to you.

Loving Your Mind and Body

VICTIMS OF SEXUAL assault or abuse often have a difficult time experiencing physical intimacy. Don't despair - many people have been able to have healthy sexual relationships even after a sexual assault; with practice, time and patience, you can be one of them. Give yourself permission to release painful stored memories to be whole again. Release energy that is not yours creating healing and a renewed sense of self.

When Amy first heard about my workshop, , she signed up immediately. She intuitively knew she had to be there. After completing the visualization exercise, Releasing Foreign Energy Time-Line Visualization, her face lit up like a midnight moon. She beamed and shared that she had been working on releasing childhood abuse memories. She said, "I found the missing puzzle piece." These memories were a major block in her life to attain intimacy with men and love herself. A week after the workshop, she met a new man and has been dating him ever since.

Your Body is an Energetic Snapshots of Your Past Love Encounters

HAVE YOU NOTICED that when involved in certain intimate relationships, your self-esteem either rises or declines? This is largely because you energetically perceive the thoughts that the significant other has of you. These thoughts may be totally unrelated to who you really are, but you begin to resonate with that energy already in your energetic field.

Have you ever been in a relationship and started to gain weight? Or lost weight when you broke up? This is because you stored large amounts

www.amirahhall.com © 2015
LOVE UP Your Life
amirah@amirahhall.com

of the other person's energy in your body. And here you thought you were just eating too much. Now that's a comforting thought!

Energetic snapshots of other people's thought forms stuck in your space or body, can block our energy flow in a particular part of your body or energy field. They create pockets of vulnerability and attract similar experiences. Other people's perceptions, thoughts and beliefs that stay in your body or energetic space eventually create dis-ease.

As a society, we are fat and, it seems, getting fatter. Excess body weight greatly reduces the feeling of being attractive and serves as a shield from sexual intimacy. It's another example of holding on to foreign energy to protect self.

Like Attracts Like

HAVE YOU NOTICED how you tend to attract the same sort of love interest in your life or the same conflicts at work? Has a traumatic sexual experience affected the type of partners you attract? Stuck energy will attract people into your life who possess similar energy or matching pictures. Maybe you completely shut off? Or do keep bringing home strays? It's not that either way is wrong or bad, it's just you will attract more of what you don't want if you don't release the stagnant energy from your space.

In order to affect change, these energetic pictures need to be de-energized, illuminated, destroyed or replaced. In fact, you attract people into your life with matching energy to create the opportunity to work through these energetic blocks. As you learn to affect energetic changes, other people's energy won't control you. If everything was always harmonious and hunky-dory in your life, it doesn't cause you to grow. Pain, challenges and difficulty in relationships motivate you to create changes.

Creating Room for Increased Sexual Expression

IS THERE IS stored up guilt within you about sex? Is sex an important part of your life? Does work or other activities overcrowd your schedule so that you don't have time to express loving sexuality?

You can begin to send an intentional energetic message into your world that you plan to break this pattern. As you begin to release the energetic charge from past mistakes, healing and changes can occur.

You Are Born With Sex Appeal

SEXUAL ENERGY IS the life force energy within you. It is at the very core of your energy bodies and the way it operates. Since the whole universe is kept together by the energy of Love, when that energy properly flows in your body, you are happy and healthy. Your whole body turns into a lighthouse, promoting good health and longevity.

Early Childhood Ideas of Sex

AS YOUNG PEOPLE, we get information about sex and sexuality from a wide range of sources. You might have discussed sex with your friends at school or from books. The media sends messages in advertising on television, in magazines and on the internet. Some of this will be accurate and some inaccurate.

You might have absorbed others' thoughts and ideas without even knowing it. These feelings might be stored deep within you and might affect your life today. Maybe a friend gave you some wrong information about sex that you accepted as truth.

It's a normal and a natural process for children to explore their sexuality during play. Were you judged by a parent, school teacher, or babysitter about innocently exploring your sexuality?

What were your parents' views about sex? Maybe you walked in on them and they were surprised. Were you resentful towards your parents because they had sex? Maybe you are holding on to some religious beliefs that are limiting you.

Did someone tell you it is wrong to be sexual or exercise your attractiveness?

Have Healthy Sexual Relationships

UNRESOLVED CONFLICT OR unexpressed anger can definitely put a damper on desire, as can negative feelings, secrets or emotional upset. If you carry around negative feelings about your partner, your level of attraction for that person can wane dramatically, sometimes never to return.

Sex is an important part of your life and your relationship. It's essential that you enjoy it. Energetically releasing conflict, anger and negative feelings will clear the path to renewed intimacy with yourself and your partners.

Releasing Foreign Energy Time-Line Visualization

THESE THOUGHTS OR negativity can be affecting you now and you can begin to release it by using the following technique.

1. Create a grounding cord for yourself.

2. Imagine a time line in front of you a time line from birth to your current age.

3. Create a mark for every year of your life on the time line.

4. Allow a dark spot to appear on the time line for every negative experience or for other peoples' thoughts you collected and absorbed.

5. Create an absorbing rose or other symbol at the beginning of the time line.

6. Slide this absorbing symbol along the time line allowing it to pull out all the dark spots of memories, negative experiences and foreign energy from each year on the time line. Let the symbol get bigger and bigger as it absorbs all the dark spots on the time line.

7. When you have absorbed all the spots on the time line and the symbol reaches the end – move the symbol out in front of you and let it explode like fireworks. Replenish your energy with a gold sun. Imagine reclaiming your liberated energy and fill up your aura and your body with your own energy.

Self Love Tip # 7

The absorbing symbol might stop along several places on the time line in order to get all the spots. Allow your symbol to clean out subconscious thoughts and hidden blocks in the energy field. Let the symbol absorb energy from any painful experiences you are ready to release.

Exploding the symbol is a way of de-energizing these experiences and taking the power out of them so they don't have power over you. You don't have to know what specific thoughts or energy to release them. Now that you have dislodged blocks of emotional pain, are you ready to let go of energy from your first time sexual experience.

CHAPTER FIVE

Release Energy from Past Sex Encounters

*W*hat concepts and energy are you still holding on to from the first time you had sex? What thoughts come to mind when you hear the words 'virginity' or 'losing your virginity'? Were you feeling fearful, disappointed, angry, excited or happy? Was it a good experience, bad or so-so experience?

Whatever that experience was there is a tremendous release of energy the first time you had sex. In addition, you stored large amounts of energy from the first time you had sex. In this chapter you will learn how to release energy stored from your first and other past sexual experiences. Then your vital energy can attract dynamic love and sex in your relationships.

The Power of Sex

SOCIETY'S VIEWS MEN losing their virginity as claiming their power. Losing virginity for women is not seen as the "proof of adulthood" that it is for men. It can actually seem for most women as genuine loss of power or independence.

Your First Sexual Experience

SADLY, MANY PEOPLE regret their first sexual experiences. Overall, women are twice as likely as men to regret it.

Diane, another Get Better Love and More of It workshop attendee, shared that she was abused as a child. Sex was a big issue for her. In her heart, Diane felt sex was a special experience to be shared by two people and yet she had a hard time connecting with her partner. She left the workshop knowing she could release feelings from her first sexual experience to gain improved sexual intimacy.

Losing your virginity is not quite like losing a set of house keys that you can have copies made. What does 'losing your virginity' mean to you? Is it a state of mind or a specific act? Is it something that can be taken from you? When does "fooling around" end and "having sex" begin?

Was your first sexual experience like rare chocolate or a once in a life time sunset? Were you traumatized and detached? For most people, the first sexual experience is embossed in their memory. Reflecting back on that moment, you will remember vivid details that surprise you. What were you thinking or feeling the first time you had sex?

Karen, another workshop participant shared her first sexual experience. She remembered trying not to laugh, as the boy seemed to take the experience seriously. She said that the experience changed her boundaries and didn't feel like having sex again until at least a year later. It wasn't until she was eighteen with my third partner that she realized that sex was meant to be fun.

www.amirahhall.com © 2015
LOVE UP Your Life

amirah@amirahhall.com

First Love Memories

CAN YOU REMEMBER your first kiss? This can be a life-transforming experience. Were you with a complete smooch goof? Was it like making out with an Electolux power nozzle? Or was it tender and maybe juicy?

Can you recall the first time you fell in love?

> *"First romance, first love, is something so special to all of us, both emotionally and physically, that it touches our lives and enriches them forever."*
>
> Rosemary Rogers

> *"First love is a little foolish and a lot of curiosity."*
>
> George Bernard Shaw

Do you remember the first time you enjoyed sex? Other than ordinary sex, you may have experiences that are far more significant to you. What was special to you?

> *"You never know where the hell you are. I keep making up these sex rules for myself, and then I break them right away."*
>
> Holden Caulfield, The Catcher in the Rye, by J.D. Salinger

Do you recall your first orgasm? Perhaps you know someone who has never had one. Was it hotter than hot? Or have to have it right now sex??? Or was it over before you could count to ten?

Emotional Component of Sex

IF YOU HAD an uncomfortable first sexual experience it may make you less willing to explore what you want now. Maybe you don't remember feeling anything during the experience. The whole experience might be a blur. Maybe you wanted that moment to be over and done with.

Does that sexual experience still count? If you haven't thought about it in years, does it mean it's not affecting you now?

Were you in a hurry to lose your virginity thinking you were ready to explode? Or did you think that if you didn't lose your virginity by a certain age you might end up an old maid? Maybe you were afraid of another person dominating you? Did you feel as though you had no personal choice and you were a victim?

At a recent workshop, Jean shared her personal story. At 15 years old, she was sexually attacked. Although, she was not actually raped, she felt her innocence and "purity" was taken away from her. Jean felt dirty and robbed. It was as if a part of her had been stolen, never to be regained.

Social Stigmas of Sex

YOUR FAMILY VALUES and religious beliefs influence your sexual beliefs and attitudes. For generations, women have been subjected to name calling. Religion put the fear of God in their young minds. Words like slut and loose woman are words used to describe women who have lost their virginity without the sacrament of marriage. Philippine culture refers to a woman who engages in premarital sex as pokpok. This means she is worn out and lost her body's freshness after several sexual encounters.

The existence and continued use of such words shows prevailing social attitudes regarding virginity and single young women: they go together like a horse and carriage.

www.amirahhall.com © 2015
LOVE UP Your Life   amirah@amirahhall.com

Conflicting Pressures

MAYBE YOUR RELIGIOUS beliefs conflict with your true feelings. Did you think you lost your purity or you were tainted? The principal sources of influence on sexuality are your parents, family, peer groups, the school, and the church. What they allow or forbid, teach, and their examples strongly influenced your sexual behavior.

Your feelings about the first time you had sex, might not be related to the act of having sex, but are based more on a social stigma. The expressions, "Men don't like women who have been had by other men" or "If you're still a virgin, then you're obviously sexually repressed" may have influenced your actions.

Reclaim Your Emotions

TO QUOTE THE song "Toyland" from the 1903 musical Babes in Toyland, "Once you pass its borders, you can never return again." Although, your virginity may be lost, reclaim your emotional energy to bolster your present loving experiences.

> **Self Love Tip # 8**
>
> **Reclaim your emotional energy from every partner and past sexual experiences.**

www.amirahhall.com © 2015
LOVE UP Your Life

amirah@amirahhall.com

No Energy for Sex

THE STRONG DESIRE for sex you experienced in your youth often takes a huge nose dive as life's responsibilities pile up. Between work, kids, friendships, school, hobbies, volunteer work, homemaking and exercise, there just doesn't seem to be time for sex. When you do get a minute of free time, often the last thing you want to do is spend it in an amorous cuddle. Watching TV, reading a good book or stealing a few extra minutes of sleep can seem so much more gratifying.

Is it any wonder that one in five American women have hypoactive sexual desire disorder more commonly referred to as low sex drive. According to Psychology Today, 40-50% of women duck out of sex. This 'headache thing' seems to be as American as apple pie.

One of America's best-kept secret is that at least 20-25% of adult males have a low desire for sex. Men are so ashamed of speaking up about low sexual desire because it violates their own sense of masculinity.

Energetically speaking, over time, foreign energy suppresses your natural sexual desire until it becomes foreign to even you. Little by little, energy from your day crowds out your natural sexual desires.

It's not that there is NO time; it's that you haven't made the time. Maybe you haven't made time because your calendar is so filled with activities and your energy space is maxed out with everyone else's energy. It might not be that you don't want to have sex; it is just because the energy you would normally use for sex, it squeezed out by other energy.

To Have it, to Lose it, to Prize or Detest it

THAT'S FINE. NONE of us knew precisely what we wanted from day one, and we are all students of life - - the curious ones, the nervous, the impatient and enthusiastic, or the frightened - all deserve to have their questions answered without fear of being called slutty or laughed at for being "repressed."

Without judgment of your first experience, as you reclaim your emotional energy from that first sexual experience, you have more energy to create magical moments. When Jessika, released emotional energy from her first sexual experience, she noticed she had more energy. She felt renewed and overall 'lighter'. To her surprise, she was holding on to a lot more energy than she would have thought she was. That experience was so far behind her, she could not imagine it still affected her life.

How to Release Energy from First Sexual Experience Visualization

IN THIS EXERCISE, give yourself permission to 'express, feel and release' any old thoughts and feelings from your first sexual encounter.

1. With eyes closed, visualize a rose or other symbol "6" in front of you.

2. Imagine that the rose or symbol is a secret friend with whom you can share your inner most thoughts.

3. Silently tell this rose or symbol everything and all about your experience. Let it absorb the negative energy or thoughts you are ready to release.

4. Imagine your communication going into the rose/symbol. When you have said everything you wish to say, imagine the rose exploding like fireworks out in front of you.

5. Replenish yourself with a gold sun showering you with your own freed up energy.

"We never forget those who make us blush."

Jean-François De La Harpe

As you release the emotions and thoughts from your first sexual experiences, you create freedom to be more present. You invite new loving sexual experiences and intimacy. Releasing emotional burdens from the past increases your vitality that increases your attractiveness.

Have you wondered why some guys have all the luck? Or maybe how some women get flowers and presents from their dates? Are you ready to have your natural charm activated to draw compliments, support, appreciation and love? In the next chapter, you will how you can be a love and sex magnet.

www.amirahhall.com © 2015
LOVE UP Your Life

amirah@amirahhall.com

CHAPTER SIX

Activate Your Love and Sex Magnetism

*a*re you ready to make potent first impressions? Why are some people naturally magnetic while other people frighten small children and dogs? In this chapter, learn how you can crank up your magnetic love energy by releasing energy from the entire body. Release stuck energy from your entire body to heal yourself, improve self-esteem, increase your libido and become a sex magnet.

Heal Your Spirit and Your Spirit Heals Your Body

IT IS NORMAL to have a healthy sex drive. Yet reports reveal that 40% of American women suffer from some form or sexual dysfunction and 23% report sexual abuse. The abundant TV and radio commercials for Cialis and Viagra point to record highs of erectile dysfunction in men.

Energetically speaking, blocked energy creates dysfunction. If you release energetic blocks from your body; your spirit heals. As you heal your spirit, your spirit often heals your body. Depression, stress, anger, guilt, anxiety and fear of sexual failure contribute to energetic blocks that can result in sexual dysfunction and dis-ease.

Stress, Fear and Anxiety Block Satisfying Sex

WHEN YOU EXPERIENCE stress, fear or anxiety, sex is usually the last thing on your mind. Work dilemmas, relationship woes, family issues and money problems can be devastating to your libido. It's hard to feel sexy when you are worried about the mortgage payment. Fear and anxiety associated with sex itself can also be problematic. Worrying about everything from STDs to fear of pregnancy to sexual performance, dampen your sex drive and hampering your chances to have a satisfying sexual experience.

Fear, anxiety and depression about aging can also affect your sex drive. Are you worried about getting older?

Stuck Energy Causes Depression

ACCORDING TO MEDICAL experts, depression is caused by an imbalance of brain chemicals, along with other factors. Energetically speaking, the root cause of depression stems from foreign energy being stuck in your body. When foreign energy dims and over-shadows your energy, you become de-pressed!

Do you remember being attracted to someone special in your life? You are attracted to someone because you admire something unique about them. You might think they are handsome, funny or even poised. You like how you feel around them. With every passing day, you start to adopt their energy as your own. When this happens, and you don't release it back to them, your own energy becomes de-pressed and your relationship takes a nose-dive.

www.amirahhall.com © 2015
LOVE UP Your Life

amirah@amirahhall.com

Like with computers, you cannot use MAC software in a PC or vice-verse. They each require their own unique software to operate and process their functions. The same is true for people. The very vibe that attracted you to another person, is the very thing that makes you sexually non-responsive, argumentative and emotional. It can affect your attitude, your health and your libido.

Depression Affects Sex Life

DEPRESSION HAS BECOME a frighteningly common diagnosis over the last few decades. In addition to making you listless, drowsy, sad, angry, upset and emotional, depression can have a profound effect on your sex life - as many as 75% of people with depression report a loss of sex drive.

Anti-depressants prescribed by many doctors to relieve depression often times decreases the libido. Medication will not help prior sexual abuse issues, body images or guilt about sex from religious programming. Ironically, the very drugs used to treat depression can also cause additional sexual dysfunctions.

Viagra Doesn't Work On Low Self Esteem

VIAGRA ONLY INCREASES blood flow to the genital area to enhance physical sexual stimulation in women or men. It cannot affect your body image, relationship or emotional issues that impede sexual function.

Most people dislike some aspect of his or her body. Do you think you have jiggly thighs, a curved penis, small breasts, fat belly or a hairy back? While you might not be 100% satisfied with the way you look, you have learned to live with the perceived flaw. This perception may actually create an energetic block that affects the sexual image of yourself and your ability to express yourself. The reality is however, that to have good feelings about sex, you have to have good feelings about your body.

Release Negative Self Talk with Grounding

WHENEVER YOU FIND yourself having a negative thought about your body, release it down your grounding cord or put it inside a symbol and explode it. For example, if you're obsessing on your extra roll of belly fat, stop yourself. Throw that thought down your grounding cord or explode inside a firecracker. Then fill yourself up with a shimmering gold sun of self-appreciation and sex appeal.

As you start to feel better about yourself and feel a little sexy - no matter what you look like - your sex drive will improve. Learn to love yourself for who you are, warts and all. Only then will you be able to have a really satisfying sex life and magnetically draw people who love and appreciate you.

Sex is an Important Part of an Adult Relationship

IF YOU DON'T have a partner, you might want to create time or space in your life to attract Mr. or Ms. Wonderful. Energy from your past partners and experiences can unconsciously occupy and create blocks to attract a new partner. Now that's a jaw dropper!

www.amirahhall.com © 2015
LOVE UP Your Life

amirah@amirahhall.com

If you have been with your current partner for many years, you have accumulated energy from the past that hinders fresh and vibrant moments. When you clear out the garage, you create room to park the car. Clear some activities off your calendar that stop you from having time for intimacy. If 40 scheduling sex into your calendar makes you giggle - do it any way! Judy shared that her partner arranges to get together 3-4 times per week. They call it their 'pre-breakfast' arrangement.

Designate time to spend quality romantic time with your partner. If you don't have a partner, clear your energy and de-stress yourself to allow room in your life to attract a desirable person.

Sexual Dysfunction and Disorders

PEOPLE WHO HAVE suffered from sexual abuse, neglect, abuse, or extreme disappointment in intimate relationships often develop some disorder of their reproductive system. Karen, a former client, had infection in her female reproductive organs. She used several of the releasing techniques from this book to release foreign energy from her organs. She saw dark colors coming out of her body and another person's face in her mind's eye. She recognized it as her first husband who was abusive to her. When she released the energies her infection cleared up.

www.amirahhall.com © 2015
LOVE UP Your Life

amirah@amirahhall.com

Criticism Lowers Self Esteem and Libido

WHEN WOMEN CRITICIZE their man, his libido takes a nose dive. Many men today are angry at their wives and are having less sex from their partner and may wander.

A high-powered male attorney client once shared that he isn't interested in having sex with his wife because she thought he worked too much. This fault finding hurt his feelings. Her criticism leads him to even more work.

Couples are working hard in the office. And women are working hard too - at home and at work. Women act like bitches and fire-hose their negativity to their partner. This negative energy emasculates and shuts off sexual desire as quickly as a terrorist attack.

When one partner yearns for more physical closeness and touch, and the other spouse is too preoccupied, too stressed or too angry, it's a big deal. The sex-starved marriage or relationship is really all about feeling wanted and appreciated.

Make Your Sexuality Your Business

TO CHANGE HOW you feel, take action. Start with yourself and your body. As the Italians say, the appetite comes while eating.

You will feel much more wanted, and more committed to the relationship when you involve yourself in attending to your sexual desires and needs. Miraculously, your partner becomes happy. You might even notice that your partner begins to do things without being asked. Both people get more of what they want.

If you are not in a current relationship or have a steady partner, you will attract one if you want one. Promise!

56

Grounding Visualization for the Entire Body

TO EXPERIENCE SELF-LOVE and appreciation, release energy by grounding the entire body. Your natural magnetic energy will be stimulated, kicking you into high gear.

1. Create a grounding cord.

2. Visualize a 2nd grounding cord from the bottom of your feet attached to the main grounding cord coming out from your spine.

3. Allow gravity to pull out any dark colors, white light or any colors you intuitively know are not your energy and need to be pulled out.

4. Release anything that prevents healing.

5. Ground your ankles, legs, knees, thighs, hips, and abdomen. Release any energy stored in those body parts.

6. Ground your sex organs. Ask yourself, "Is there anyone's energy stored there?" Do you get a sense of thoughts or judgments from: former teachers, lovers, partners, or friends sitting on your skin or inside these areas? Release both positive and negative energies. If someone likes the shape of your butt, their energy stays with it. And, here you thought it was because of all of the chocolate you ate.

7. Replenish your body and organs with a golden sun by putting some of your own energy back in your body.

Self Love - SECRET TIP # 9

Positive or negative energy can also block the optimum energy function.

Stuck Molestation Energy

MOST PEOPLE HAVE some form of molestation in their past. Sexual abuse and incest occur in every race, class, religion, culture, and country. Every two and a half minutes, somewhere in America, someone is sexually assaulted. One in six American women has been the victim of an attempted or completed rape, and 10% of sexual assault victims are men.

Contrary to the belief that offenders are hiding in the bushes or in the shadows of the parking garage, almost two-thirds of all sexual offenses were committed by someone known to the person. 67% of sexual assaults were perpetrated by a non-stranger.

An individual who has been sexually abused can be vulnerable to being sexually abused again. The energetic imprint that is left in the body or emotions will attract more of the same until it has been released.

You may not have been physically molested to have stored abusive sexual energy in your body. A distant relative or an adult may thought of you in an inappropriate manner and the energy may be stored in your emotional energetic center.

Sexual thoughts from others may have turned off your own feminine or masculine energy when you were a child. Even if you are not aware of this, it's important to clear out any foreign energy you may have from your energetic space.

What is Past is Past!

DON'T GET STUCK ON it. Allow past energy release. It's no fun to be stuck in the past. It's no fun to be a victim. Stay present so you can let go, move on and attract the type of loving relationship you desire. You can release the emotional charge of molestation through Visualization.

www.amirahhall.com © 2015
LOVE UP Your Life

amirah@amirahhall.com

Releasing Molestation Visualization

IMAGINE AN ABSORBING rose that will attract all energy relating to molestation or inappropriate thoughts from your body and aura. As you release this energy, you will begin to attract and an abundance of love and appreciation.

1. Create a yellow rose in front of you.

2. Imagine that it is programmed to pull out any inappropriate thoughts from adults around you when you were growing up.

3. Let these thoughts appear in your mind's eye throughout the aura as little purple dots.

4. Visualize these little purple dots being vacuumed into the yellow rose.

5. When the rose is filled with all the purple dots, allow it to explode like fireworks discharging the energy of any of those stuck thoughts.

6. Replenish energy by creating a magnetic gold sun that pulls back more of your life force energy.

7. Allow the sun to enter the top of your head filling the entire body and the aura with your own life force energy. Imagine your energy coming back to you.

FACT

Whether you are aware of an experience or not, it does NOT matter nor affect the outcome.

59

Self Love - SECRET TIP # 10

The magic of 'Releasing Molestation Visualization' is that you DO NOT have to re-live every experience to release it.

What is a Normal Sex Drive?

IF YOU'RE FRUSTRATED about your lack of sexual appetite, go easy on yourself. Everyone's body is different. There is no "normal" level of sex drive. Your personal sense of normalcy is defined by how you feel about your sexuality and whether or not you're happy with how you express it. If you're one of the lucky people who are perfectly comfortable with his or her sexuality, congratulate yourself.

Ensure a Healthy Body and Love Life

LEARN TO RELEASE stress, fear and anxiety to ensure a healthy body. Eat a balanced diet, drink plenty of water, sleep at least eight hours a night, exercise regularly and practice relaxation techniques such as meditation or yoga. If you won't do it for your general health, do it for your sex life!

Do you wonder what your natural attractive force feels like? Did you ever feel that you had what it takes to get all the sex you wanted? Get ready to re-create more intimacy, attracting more attention that just might surprise you. Unlock the powerful attractive force within.

CHAPTER SEVEN

Unlock Your Natural Attractive Force

*D*o you dream of finding and keeping a perfect relationship? What if you are in a partnership that is confusing and always changing? Are you attracting any kind of intimate interactions at all? The working dynamics of good relationships are for many of us one of the greatest mysteries of life. It is a secret many of us seek to unravel. Others have simply given in to being alone. In this chapter, you learn to access and balance your own unique vibration of energy to reveal your innate power and beauty within to attract the type of relationships you desire.

Attract the Right Relationship

YOU ARE OUT of balance if you forget who you are, or are afraid to accept yourself. As long as you resist being your natural, balanced self, you will not attract harmonious, long lasting, or healthy relationships. Once you become true to yourself, you automatically attract the right person to you.

When someone decides to change or leave a relationship it is because their energy is no longer in harmony with yours. When you understand this, nothing will really be missing. We cannot miss anything from a vibration that we are not truly a part of. Isn't that comforting?

www.amirahhall.com © 2015
LOVE UP Your Life

amirah@amirahhall.com

What Do You Really Want?

WE HAVE ALL been told from birth what to do and what not to do. We follow rules because we want to live in harmony. But, along the way we are also told by parents, teachers, advisors, and bosses what we "should" and "should not" do to suit their personal agendas and perspectives. These "shoulds" program you. When you continually try to follow them and get confusing and mixed results.

Your inner passions develop early in life, and change with time. Yet you suppress them. These passions are almost always good in nature and positive. You may have a passion to create a rose garden or to play the drums, but don't. You may not recognize or accept your passions. If you did, your conscious mind would rationalize that you "shouldn't" after responding to all of the previously implanted "shoulds" by others. Yet, you may feel something is missing and can't put a finger on it.

Your Desires Are Important

YOUR DESIRES ARE important. You want to stay healthy, feel secure, eat and have a roof over your head. These basic desires are rather easy to determine. Once you recognize they exist, you understand they are required for a full existence.

Once you accomplish these desires, you develop other desires. You may desire to live in a warm climate, work outdoors, raise a happy and healthy family, and be acknowledged for being special. These personal desires are less obvious and more personal in nature.

This is where the "shoulds" begin to enter the picture, and you find yourself following the desires you allow others to impose on you. For example, you might go to law school to become a lawyer because your parents strongly felt you "should" become a lawyer. Or you might become a full-time mom and raise a family early on in life because that is what everyone did where you grew up.

You Broadcast Who You Are and What You Want

WHAT YOU THINK about, you attract. When you are cautious and hold back your true self, you attract similar situations to you. If you think you are not sufficient, not wise enough, or not powerful enough to create the reality you truly desire, you will attract a representation of your own doubt in yourself.

Terry secretly wanted to be a writer. She wrote poems and short stories but never felt they were good enough to share with the world. She also wanted to write a book but she recalled her mother thought she should direct her energy to getting a good job. Recently, she wrote a poem that reflected her hidden feelings that her mother had cursed her from expressing her true passion. She unconsciously knew that the energy of her mother's thoughts and beliefs suppressed her passion to pursue her dream to be a writer. Unconsciously, her energy broadcasted to the world that she was unsuccessful and downtrodden.

Remember, the vibration you are is what you broadcast to the world. You receive more of what you put out. There are no exceptions.

63

You Are Worthy of Quality Partners

WHAT IS THE quality of your relationship with yourself? Do you know who you are? What do you like? Do you believe you are worthy and deserve unconditional love?

While you may know how you would like someone to love you, do you love yourself that way already? Do you trust and accept all parts of yourself? When you look in the mirror do you like what you see? Do you like your income? The bottom line is that you simply want to be loved and accepted for who you are, for your real self.

Attract Balanced Relationships

MOST PEOPLE FUNCTION as if only half complete. If you project the vibration of half and you look for someone else to complete you, you attract an incomplete relationship.

When you have a viewpoint that a relationship will complete you, you attract more incompleteness. What you create is a partnership made up of two half people, that will not satisfy either person.

When you feel complete and sufficient, you set up a vibration that attracts those with the similar qualities. Have you written a long, wonderful list of attributes you wish your dream partner to have? Ask yourself, "Are you all those things? Do you have all those attributes?

When you reflect the type of vibrations you choose to attract in someone else, you will be seen and recognized by Mr./Ms. Wonderful.

Create Your Natural Balance

EVERYONE HAS A natural balance of male and female energy within. The proportions of male and female energy that you use are unique to who you are. Continuously bombarded with other people's energies, opinions, attitudes, judgments, criticisms, and negativity, your natural balance of male and female energy gets readjusted or turned off.

This imbalance dims your natural attractive force. If you are a woman, once you tap into your pure feminine, you unlock your natural attractive force within. If you are a man, once you tap into your pure masculine energy, you unlock your natural attractive force within.

Re-ignite Your Attractive Power

BALANCING YOUR OWN male or female energy is easy. When you flood your body with your own female or male energy, your body automatically seeks its original perfect balance. With practice your system will stay in balance effortlessly. This way you can experience your ultimate sexual and creative power.

Cleanse Your Creative Energy

IF YOU ARE a woman, it's beneficial to cleanse and purify your female energy. If you are a man, it's beneficial to cleanse and purify your male energy. Cleansing your own creative energy helps to differentiate your energy from everyone else's energy in your body and space. It cleanses foreign energy from your space so that you can run the optimum amounts of male and female energy that are unique to you.

Heal Your Self to Heal Others

MAYBE YOU HAVE heard it said, "If you want to heal the planet, heal yourself." As you balance the energy within yourself, you affect everything around you. In healing yourself, you heal others and the planet. With focus on yourself and how you feel, you will heal your partner, spouse, children, family and friends. Unconsciously, others will give themselves permission to balance themselves as well.

On the spiritual and physical level, when you cleanse foreign energy stuck inside you increase your sexual, emotional, creative and attractive power. It removes impurities and negative influences that diffuse your innate power and vitality. As you release male or female invalidation, media, family, religious, programming, secrets, and societal influences, you free yourself to become familiar with your own frequency. Your attractive force will be transformed.

> ### Self Love TIP #11
>
> **Let your own female or male energy cleanse out any stuck thoughts.**

After just one practice dramatic improvements can occur. The more you practice however, the better the results.

Become Clear and Certain About What You Want

CONNECTING WITH YOUR innate power and sexual force spawns a new level of self certainty. Your confidence will soar and you may find yourself achieving goals you long forgot. As you get neutral and get rid of foreign energies that compete for space in your body, you become clear, grounded and focused.

Your Creative Essence is Attractive

AS YOU CONNECT with your own creative energy, you access true inner power and beauty. It is empowering to access your own sexual vibration. People will respond favorably and may wonder what secret you are guarding.

> *"What lies behind us and lies before us are small matters to what lies within us. And when we bring what is within out into the world, miracles happen"*
>
> Henry David Thoreau

Achieve Life Balance

PEOPLE ACHIEVE BALANCE in their lives when they can consciously and subconsciously align their thoughts and activities with who they are and what they want to do, without conflict or guilt. When you are in balance, you experience "being in the zone" of life. Life is good!

As you release conflicting forces or energies of what others want you to do, you re-connect with your true passions and desires. If you've ever tried you know how tricky this can be. You will be relieved! You will function better on a daily basis and feel motivated to do even the most mundane tasks. Conflicts will be minimized and life will flow much easier.

Follow Your Own Path

LIFE IS A journey, and you have everything you need to create the most desirable, enjoyable and fulfilling journey for yourself. Take steps each day to reach your life goals, and you will not only be amazed at how well you will achieve them, but at how enjoyable and stress-free the journey will be.

Your desires, priorities, passions, and even sometimes your beliefs will change. That is very normal. Once you discover what your new ones are, you will want to create new goals accordingly, using the same process and continue life's journey in the new directions that you choose for yourself.

Your Attractive Force Within IS Powerful

YOUR RENEWED PERSONAL power will revolutionize your relationships. People around you will notice a positive change in you. They may not put their finger on it but you will know why they respond favorably.

Jennie, a former student, was significantly overweight and had not been on a date for several years. On her way home after class she stopped at the store to buy some groceries. A man approached her and complimented her and asked her out on a date. He made a comment that he found her attractive and that he thought she would be good in bed too.

Jennie didn't accept his invitation but she was flattered and dumbfounded on the amazing response she received from the shift in her energy. She also went on to create a lasting a fulfilling relationship with another man.

Everyone has both male and female energies. Sometimes someone from your past has turned off your male or female energy. It affects how and what you attract in your life. In the following exercise, you will increase the amount of female or male energy running in your body to increase your sex appeal and attraction.

Self Love TIP #12

Practice this energy technique for 20-30 days and the results will astonish you.

Increase Your Natural Sex Appeal with Visualization

TO YOUR OWN natural attractive energy, to increase your own sexual energy and allow it to flow throughout your body. Listen to Creating Clarity Guided Meditation - Quantum Energy Tool #2 - https://www.youtube.com/watch?v=D9AUFo14IBc 1.

1. Close your eyes, but stay focused.

2. Visualize yourself sitting in a control room in the center of your head where you have command of your entire being.

3. In your mind's eye, visualize a scale or gauge from 0-100% that represents your current male or female energy running in your body. Notice the current reading of your meter. Don't judge it. Just note what you see.

4. Imagine increasing this energy by slowly raising your gauge to 100%. If you have a female body, allow your female energy to rise to 100%. If you have a male body, allow your male energy to rise to 100%.

5. Simultaneously, allow the energy from the sexual center, approximately 2" below your navel, begin to move throughout the entire body. Breath in from the navel and imagine the energy flowing upwards through the torso, down the arms, and up into the head. Allow this sexual energy flow out the top of your head

like a fountain. Let the energy flow down to your feet and bring the energy up through the bottoms of your feet, into the legs creating a cycle of your own flowing feminine or masculine energy.

6. Choose a color for this energy flowing through the body as you push the needle on the gauge to 100%.

7. Allow yourself to experience your powerful male or female energy flushing out foreign energies from your body. Let this energy flow for about 5 minutes. Notice how your body feels.

8. Allow your system to adjust to a level where you feel most comfortable.

In this chapter, you discovered you can increase your natural sex appeal by connecting with and increasing the flow your own feminine or masculine energy. When you run your own energy you increase self-confidence, boost your attractiveness and create balance.

Do you want to create more supportive relationships? Are you ready to release programming that keep you feeling apathetic about your life passions? Are you ready to have more vibrant, fulfilling and passionate sexual experiences? In chapter eight, learn how to stimulate the body's largest sexual center – The Brain!

www.amirahhall.com © 2015
LOVE UP Your Life
amirah@amirahhall.com

CHAPTER EIGHT

Stimulate Your Largest Pleasure Center

*I*s Your "Libido Meter" High or Low? Are you having fewer satisfying intimate moments with your partner lately? Does your partner have a higher sex drive than you? Do you even have a sex life? In this chapter, learn how stuck thoughts and foreign energy in the brain can block your body's ability to access these pleasure centers.

It may now be a cliché, but it is no less true—the most important sexual organ is the brain. Sex is one of the strongest innate drives in all organisms. The survival of the species depends on it.

Sexual Pleasure Gives Meaning and Purpose to Your Life

SEX IS PROBABLY at the top of the hierarchy of natural pleasures. When you enjoy it, your state of satisfaction buffers you from stress. Your sexual energy is the source of our life force energy and a primary key to a happy life.

Good Sex is Important to Your Well Being

CHEMICALS ARE RELEASED in the brain during sex that promote emotional bonding and can reduce your heart rate and blood pressure. They provide natural relief from the pain of arthritis, injury, and even migraines. They boost the immune system by dampening the harmful hormones that stress stimulates. After good sex, generally people have a feeling of pleasure, satiety, and relaxation.

Take all of that together, and it's easy to see how pervasive sexual pleasure is to your well-being.

Increased Self Esteem

A GOOD SEXUAL relationship can have a profoundly positive impact on a person's mental health. If you feel good about your sex life, you will be more confident, happier and have higher levels of sex hormones. Can you remember a time when you were sexually fulfilled?

There is a strong link between sex and a person's psychological well-being. A person with a sexual problem often can think of nothing else. That sort of obsession often affects a person's self-esteem and causes a general increase in life stress.

Your Brain Controls Your Sex Drive

THE BRAIN CONTROLS almost all bodily functions. It's the seat of emotions, desires, drives and impulses. It's where you fall in and out of love...or lust. Having an orgasm is like getting high. By releasing a myriad of substances into your bloodstream, you are altering your brain and body functions.

www.amirahhall.com © 2015
LOVE UP Your Life

amirah@amirahhall.com

When was the last time you felt that 'sexual high'? Have you ever heard yourself saying, "is that all there is?" or "What's all the fuss about?"

Being Aroused is a Good Thing – Oh Yah!

WHEN YOU ARE aroused, your body becomes like a fine tuned automobile. Everything works better. You may even forget any pain that you have. Your heart beats faster, your blood pressure rises and you breathe deeper. You produce opiate type endorphins and all kinds of good things happen to your body.

Do you ever feel like you hold yourself back from being turned on? Are you worried about what your mother might be thinking if she saw you now? Do you fear contracting a disease, so you don't go there?

Your Brain Controls Arousal

EVER WONDER WHY you get a rush of self-confidence right after you have an orgasm? Ever wonder why you fall dead asleep or get a rush of self-confidence right after you have an orgasm? Or are you lit up like a house on fire?

Although you think everything happens between your legs, the sensation of orgasm actually originates with neuro-chemical changes in your brain. Endorphins, oxytocins and other chemicals are released from your brain into your bloodstream upon "liftoff". If there is an energetic break or foreign energy on the brain preventing it from sending an arousal signal – dysfunction occurs. It might just be a single thought that stops you from getting aroused.

♥
73

Sexual Stimulation Starts in Your Brain

THE ONSET OF sexual stimulation begins when one part of the brain, the hypothalamus, sends a signal to another part of the brain, the pituitary gland. This signal tells the pituitary gland to begin releasing hormones that stimulate sexual desire.

In a male, if he sees or reads something that excites him sexually, the brain triggers the release of hormones. A signal is transmitted from the brain to the sex organs. If there is an interruption in the transmittal – it is difficult for a man to fully get aroused.

So you can say the biggest sex organ for men is their eyes. Foreign energy can collect in the brain and the connection between the sex organs thus causing some impairment for men to get aroused.

Researchers claim many women are most stimulated by what they hear or what is said to them. Then a signal is sent to the brain to create chemicals that in turn send a signal to her sex organs. You could say the biggest sex organ in women is hearing, her ears and what she hears. Women, much more so than men, can be emotionally touched and sexually aroused by language.

Foreign energy can collect in your brain reducing or preventing the ability to produce chemicals. Additionally, it can collect on the connection between the brain and the sex organs causing sexual impairment.

Increase and Access the Body's Pleasure Center

THE BRAIN IS flooded with natural chemicals that act similarly to drugs such as cocaine. These natural chemicals, called endorphins, make you say to yourself that whatever is causing the sexual arousal is enjoyable and should be continued.

Chemicals That Fuel Your Sex Life

WITHOUT THE PRODUCTION of hormones or chemicals your libido and desire for sex may disappear. You need hormones to make you feel horny. They are responsible for a myriad of feelings including cheerfulness, enthusiasm, and relaxation. Even that "cuddling feeling" when you want to connect and bond with your lover is a result of chemicals being released in your brain.

Lower Stress and Boost Confidence

ENDORPHINS HAVE A similar chemical structure to morphine. Endorphins get your adrenaline, and other things pumping. They produce feelings of euphoria and pleasure. They fill you with a sense of well-being and relaxation. When a man passes out post-sex, it's the endorphins at work. The faster he falls asleep, the better the sex was for him. So, ladies this can be a compliment to you. In turn, women may feel so good they want to keep a good thing going.

Trigger Pleasure Centers in the Brain

PHENYLETHYLAMINE TRIGGERS THE release of dopamine in the pleasure centers of the brain. This chemical is released during sex and peaks at orgasm. Dopamine gives you that overwhelming feeling of attraction, excitement and bliss. Curiously, it is also one of the chemicals found in chocolate.

Fuels Sex Drive

TESTOSTERONE IS ESSENTIAL to your libido and sexual arousal. Both, men and women with a testosterone deficiency often have trouble getting aroused and have a lower interest in sex. In short, testosterone gets you turned on and keeps you sexually virile. If you ever noticed a rush of confidence after sex, that could be increased testosterone at work.

Serotonin Acts as an Anti-Depressant

SEROTONIN REGULATES YOUR moods. Having an orgasm releases an extra shot of serotonin to your brain, which acts as an anti-depressant. You feel cheerful, hopeful, emotionally balanced, and content. It's a natural high.

Some people go to great lengths to get drugs, but why bother when these active chemicals are just waiting to be released in your body? Clearing foreign energy that prevents their release may bring you to a new level of sexual ecstasy.

www.amirahhall.com © 2015
LOVE UP Your Life

amirah@amirahhall.com

Fantasyland

THE POET, MAYA Angelou, says...

> *"if a person is lucky, a good fantasy can displace a thousand realities".*

Fantasies are daydreams. Imaginary visions. Whimsical speculations. Wishful thinking. Everybody fantasizes at some level. If you've ever imagined what you'd do if you won the lottery, you've used fantasy.

Do fantasies expand your love life? Or do they keep you from enjoying sex with your partner? Maybe you enjoy your fantasies more than the real thing? Some people may be ashamed to admit it, but it's normal to have sexual fantasies.

Fantasizing About Other People

SOME PEOPLE WORRY that fantasizing about someone other than their partner is an act of betrayal, revealing either a desire to be unfaithful or that they are longer turned on by their partner alone.

In fact, this is very rarely the case. Evidence suggests that those who fantasize the most are in happy, loving, trusting relationships. It's in this kind of context that the mind explores places the body has no intention of visiting.

The Benefits of Fantasy

SEX GENERALLY STARTS in the brain. So an active imagination can mean you're ready for sex before anything physical has happened. Therefore, desire is heightened and arousal is much quicker. Some people find an active fantasy life can add novelty to a long-standing sexual relationship. This can be particularly helpful if your partner is not as sexually adventurous as you are.

Some Fantasies May Be Borrowed

IT'S NOT A question of whether you have fantasies or not, or how fantastic they are or not. Some of the fantasies may not even be your own. Maybe you borrowed them from a movie or a former lover. If you feel the need to make it a reality, your fantasy could bring you harm.

Self Love TIP #13

Give your imagination free rein and to play. Shift your sexual fantasies by clearing foreign energy from your brain. They may become more alive, realistic or completely change.

Susan had a sexual fantasy of making love to a stranger in a dark park. Every week she would stroll through the park imagining this stranger coming out from the dark and having mad passionate sex with him. What she didn't realize is that she was putting herself in jeopardy of being raped and maybe murdered. This was not a fantasy that would enhance or create a positive experience.

Many women fantasize about being strippers, while others take things a step further and imagine being prostitutes. Obviously, the fantasy is romanticized beyond belief because the life of either is not so glamorous that women would opt to have it as a career choice. Many men fantasize about being with two women or having a woman totally in control of him.

Fantasies can enhance, rather than harm, a relationship. As you know yourself better, you are free to celebrate your natural erotic rhythms with whatever thoughts quicken your pulses and please your heart.

Clearing Foreign Energy in the Brain Visualization

INCREASE YOUR ABILITY to enjoy increased sensual pleasures. Stimulate your brain for an increased sense of overall well being that will lead to increased sexual activity and pleasure. Release foreign energy from the brain such as beliefs, old thoughts, fears and limitations that prevent your brain from optimal function.

1. Create a grounding cord.

2. Close your eyes, but stay focused.

3. Visualize a second grounding from the entire brain to your main grounding cord.

4. Imagine siphoning off foreign energy that has been collected in the brain and releasing it into the planet.

5. Picture the foreign energy appearing as different colors draining down the grounding cord to the center of the planet.

6. When the energy is clear from the brain, visualize a shimmering gold sun producing more of your life force energy.

7. Replenish your body and brain with the golden sun.

After practicing this Visualization, Sandra noticed the frequency of informal dates increased. She received more affectionate gestures from both male and female friends. Within a week several old boyfriends showed up on her door step with intentions or rekindling old flames. With abundant sexual opportunities, she now had a new problem. Which old flame if any was she really interested in having sex with? Oh what a problem!

Self Love TIP #14

You don't have to know the exact location of any parts of your brain for these visualizations to be effective.

Activate Your Sexual Force

UNDERSTANDING THE HIDDEN power of sex, you can create a vital, fulfilling loving relationship. Your sexual organs are designed for use and enjoyment, not to be considered shameful or produce guilt. Have more fun with your partner. Or allow yourself to attract a new loving partner to play with.

A host of sexual chemicals that affect your mind and body are released during and after sex.

Use It or Lose It

YOUR BODY WILL not waste any energy that is not necessary. If you tie your arm in a sling and don't use it for six months, it will waste away to just skin and bones. The same will happen to any other part of your body.

Have you become apathetic about sex? Has it been so long since you had a sexual experience, that chocolate has become your replacement for sex?

amirah@amirahhall.com

Self Love TIP #15

If you don't have sex for some time or don't think about having it, you may lose your desire for it. If you don't use it, you lose it.

Aphrodisiacs and Potency Restorers

FOR AGES AND ages, men have looked for something that would restore their youthful sexual potency. Almost everything imaginable has been tried. The rhinoceros has almost been wiped out because some men believe that ground up rhinoceros horn will restore their potency and make them horny. Some men in the Far East believe that drinking the blood of a live snake will do the trick. And of course, men have eaten raw oysters and hundreds of other drugs and animal products in a futile attempt to regain their lost potency.

The internet bombards us with glowing ads for pills that will restore sexual potency and sexual arousal. They include dozens of testimonials from men who swear that the drugs turned them into a sex machine.

If you are looking for a natural product to enhance your libido, endurance and energy, the author personally recommends "Warrior – Amazon Herb Co." or the super food maca.

PONDER THIS:

There are consequences to taking drugs. They may pump up one part of you and dump another part of you. This may even result in long term damage that isn't reversible.

www.amirahhall.com © 2015
LOVE UP Your Life

amirah@amirahhall.com

Clearing Connections from Your Brain to Your Sex Organs Visualization

INCREASE YOUR ABILITY to be aroused. Renew your sexual pleasure. Repair the communication link between your brain and sex organs to maximize your pleasures and double your fun.

1. Visualize yourself drawing a bright blue line from the brain down to the sex organs.

2. Imagine that this connection is made between the two locations and imagine this line getting repaired.

3. Visualize a giant gold sun above your head producing more of your life force energy.

4. Replenish the body and fill the brain with a gold sun.

A Measure of Health

HAVE YOU CONSIDERED the connection between having sex and your overall physical and mental health? When you have frequent, satisfying sex keeps the hormone levels up and keeps you young, both physically and mentally. Besides being a measure of good exercise, sex improves cholesterol levels, increases circulation, and combats heart disease.

In this chapter, you learned to clear your brain of foreign energy to have more fulfilling sexual relations and emotional intimacy. Now that you have an increased sense of vitality and power, are you ready to focus your sexual energy to attract someone special?

www.amirahhall.com © 2015
LOVE UP Your Life

amirah@amirahhall.com

CHAPTER NINE

Harness and Radiate Sexual Energy

*a*re you aware when you send out sexual vibes to attract someone that interests you? Or have you shut down your sexual energy center because you have been hurt by a past partner? In this chapter, learn how to send sexual energy when you intend on attracting someone or close down this energy when you are in the business mode.

Your Sexual Energy Center

WHAT IF YOU could focus your sexual energy? Then you could follow the principle of the Martial Arts and many of the Eastern meditative practices, who have long been aware of and harnessed the body's energy centers. Most martial artists spend years learning to focus their energy to be effective and powerful. Would it be useful for you if you could get just a little of the focus and centering they have? Well you can.

Your sexual energy center is located about two inches below your naval, from the centre out to the sides. When you feel sexual desire for someone, chances are you have sensations here.

You Are a Sexual Being

WE ARE ALL sexual beings but many of us try to cover it up. Or maybe you just forgot how sexual you are. Centuries of dogmatic religions and other cultural prisons have force fed people lies about themselves. You probably learned that sex is sex and there is a time and a place for it.

In today's society, men are afraid to making a move on a woman for fear of offending her. Women are afraid to be sexual in case they are judged. Are you afraid of emotional blackmail, unwanted pregnancy, sexual fantasies, self pleasure or sexually transmitted disease?

It's not our natural or powerful state to live life with fear. This blocks your natural flow of sexual expression and attracts the very thing you fear. In a past workshop, Sherry shared she was afraid of having sexual relations because she was afraid of what her mother would think of her. She continually worried about doing the right thing in her mother's mind. This blocked her natural ability to express herself and allow men to approach her.

Fall in Love with Your Sexuality

"When passion burns within you remember that it was given to you for a good purpose."

Old Hassidic saying.

DO YOU FEEL like you lost touch with your sexuality? Or is it like a raging out of control child that wants its way all of the time? Do you continually attract partners that are destructive to your well being? Learn to celebrate your sexual energy power. Directing your sexuality as a wondrous driving force in your life can be playful and fun. Like golf, learning to fall in love with your sexuality is like learning to mastering the game. It takes practice, practice, practice. What fun that can be!

Wonderful Soulful Sex

SEXUAL ENERGY IS one of the most powerful motivating forces in your life. The urge to reproduce, is genetically imprinted within. As humans evolve, the primal drive to reproduce continues to exist but the urge to reproduce, is no longer the life and death matter it was in the past.

So what do you do with all this excess sexual energy? As well as enjoying wonderful soulful sex, ou can learn to harness and use this motivational force in other areas of your life.

Harness Your Sexual Energy

WHY WOULD ANYONE want to do that? Lots of good sex is not a bad thing right! It may be that this energy is being used in ways that create an imbalance of other parts of you. This energy center shares space with your emotional and creative expressions. If you over-express your sexuality, maybe your emotional energy is out of balance. Or maybe your concentration of sexual expression depletes your creative output.

Rosie hated ironing. When she learned to harness her sexual energy she discovered how to turn ironing into a very pleasurable task! She uses this energy to accomplish household tasks that she once resisted. Now, Rosie gets into her long black boots and not much else. She irons on and on and on.

Dominic had a challenging time working with his managers. He resented their suggestions. When he learned to direct his energy from his sexual center to his work, he became more creative and productive.

He felt good about his accomplishments. Before long, Dominic was having as much fun at work as he does with his girlfriend!

Harness your sexual energy and use it in all areas of your life. Think about how you could harness your life force.

Are you substituting sex for creativity or emotional fulfillment? Have you neglected your urge to express your creativity? Are you avoiding the emotional side of yourself? Do you use sex as a way to express another part of yourself that is closed off never to be exposed?

Wanda is a talented artist but recently felt blocked. Her resistance puzzled her. What she didn't understand is why she would stop doing what she loved the most. During our conversation, she shared that she started dating a man who demands a lot of her time and attention. As the relationship started heating up, her creative flow was interrupted. Harness your creative, emotional and sexual energy to fulfill your desires.

> *The primary nature of every human being is to be open to life and love.*
>
> Alexander Lowe

What Makes Someone Desire You Instantly?

MY FRIEND KAREN says that sometimes she walks into a room and it's like she's been hit by a 'wall of testosterone'. She senses certain men's energy radiating. Some men give it off and others don't. Some women give it off, and others don't. So what's the secret of using this energy to your advantage?

Strong Sexual Energy

MEN THAT ARE instantly sexually attractive to women radiate a masculine vibe. This doesn't mean that they are all 6ft muscle-bound animals. What they are giving out is a strong male vibration that could be described as 'confidence'. When a man is confident and self assured, it means that he is OK with who he is. Women radiate similar energy but it has a different vibration and is distinctly perceived by males as a feminine vibe. When a woman is confident and trusts herself, she is powerfully seductive. This is also described as 'confidence'.

You emit energy all the time. The maleness of men is determined by testosterone levels or the level of male energy that they generate. When the female gives off her natural estrogen, she is vibrant.

When you are happy you emit different energy and chemicals to those that you emit when you are sad. When you are depressed, your energetic vibration is 'de-pressed' with foreign energy. When you connect with your own vibrant sexual energy, you emit more sexual chemicals and attractive vibrant energy. Being attractive has nothing to do with your looks and everything to do with your vibe.

www.amirahhall.com © 2015
LOVE UP Your Life
amirah@amirahhall.com

You are a Sense-ual Being

CAN YOU RELATE to people say things like, "I just felt right about him, he had a look about him or I liked the smell of him." You sense a person's confidence, using dormant powers of sensory and energetic perception. You unconsciously pick up on sexual chemicals and energy that other people exude.

Use Your Gut Feelings

HAVE YOU EVER heard someone say they have a gut feeling about something? In addition to using the five senses, sight, smell, hearing, touch and feeling, you use your sixth sense of intuition. You perceive signs and messages inaudible to your conscious mind. You put these signs together and get a gut feeling.

You are born with perfect and accurate chemical and energy sensors. This energy center controls your emotions, sexual expression and creative output. It emits your emotions and senses to other people. They interpret the signals and react accordingly.

The gut feeling center is responsible for your sensitivity and feelings. This is the energy center that allows you to get turned on. Over time this energy center become clouded or diffused by foreign energy from parents, teachers, ex-partners, family members and friends. When your sexual center closes down, your sexuality becomes impeded. If it's wide open, you are HOT!

Sex Helps to Get in Touch With Your Emotions

SEX IS ONE of the best ways to get in touch with your emotions. Emotions that you may be stuffing down will rise on the breath, especially when sexual energy is being raised. Have you ever had an orgasm where you wound up in tears, for instance? Or got really angry? Or started laughing uncontrollably? You may have felt these emotions rise during sex, but push them down because you think they are inappropriate. Or you are afraid that your partner will be offended or frightened.

Hot to Trot? Or NOT?

> **Ponder this**
>
> Is your sexual energy center stuck wide open in lust mode? Are your primitive urges running your life into the ditch? Or is it locked down like a high security prison?

Is Your Sexual Center On or Off? Open or Closed?

WHEN SOMEONE ELSE'S energy enters the sexual energy center, it sends a signal to the brain. The brain, in turn, sends a signal to the sex organs to get aroused or turned on. If the sexual energy center is closed down, you miss the show.

You can control whether or not you get turned on by regulating this energy center. It works much like a camera lens letting light in. You can open it simply by mentally commanding it to open. Imagine the energy center opening to 100%. Open and close depending on your situation.

At 100%, your sexual vibration is released. It's easy to pick up other people's energy through this center when it's wide open. If you are at work, church, school or any place where you are in business mode, turn down the sexual center.

Self Love TIP #16

Open the sexual energy center when you want to be turned on or want to turn someone else on.

Ana practiced the techniques in this book for a week and noticed almost immediate changes. She hadn't been in a long term relationship for a while but really wants to have one. During the week, she observed she was having more fun meeting people. She felt more enthusiastic about finding someone to share her life with. Out at a single's dance party, a man approached her. When he touched her on the shoulder, she became uncomfortable. He made her feel uneasy with his sudden advances.

Rather than making a scene, she took control of the situation and closed down her sexual energy center. Almost immediately, he took his hand off her shoulder and walked away. Ana was pleased how she affected the situation so effortlessly.

Open and Close Your Sexual Energy Center Visualization

PRACTICE OPENING AND closing your sexual energy center located two inches below your navel. Then you will become familiar with the difference of how it feels to your body. With practice you can open or close it depending on the situation to attract someone to you or deflect incoming sexual vibes.

1. Imagine your focus is behind your eyes rather than having the gut feeling.

2. Bring your attention to the point about 2" below the navel.

www.amirahhall.com © 2015
LOVE UP Your Life

amirah@amirahhall.com

3. Envision your sexual energy center opening up like a camera lens.

4. Allow your sexual energy to release. Notice what happens.

5. Imagine closing down the energy center, picture closing down emotions and sexuality. Notice what happens and how it feels to your body.

6. Allow your sexual energy center to adjust to a level that feels comfortable to you.

A lot of time, when your love life is getting hot – you've had your sexual center open.

Primitive Sexual Response

IN THE PRIMITIVE beginning of humans, women and men were programmed to fulfill certain roles. A man's purpose was to spread his seed and a woman's purpose was to find a man to impregnate her and take care of business while she nurtured the child.

Despite passing time, these primary drivers, continue to organize our sexual direction. It's what some call the primitive urge. That's why men do sometimes yearn to stray and women feel their biological clocks ticking.

You are not your primitive ancestors. Although you have evolved, many layers remain cloaking your primitive sexuality. Essentially, you are a sexual being driven by primary urges. A woman may feel the urgency of finding a mate and start a family. A man may feel the call to work and propagate.

It's Time to Take Tarzan and Jane Out of the Jungle

OVER CENTURIES, THE brain has evolved and society has harnessed nature and technology. Women defy nature by establishing careers. Men are not always the providers or towers of strength that society depicts them as. Today, people have choices in the role they play in a male or female relationship.

In a survey of successful career women, scientists registered quite elevated levels of testosterone. Energetically, women are running more male than female energy through their bodies. This creates an imbalance in their original sexual blue-print and diffuses their true feminine power.

Studies show that men are experiencing lowered sperm counts which could be the result of running more female energy in their bodies, confusing their own sexual blue-prints.

Studies may be enlightening but they aren't the whole truth.

Time marches on and the link to our primitive sexual roots is evident in our ongoing desire to mate, copulate, have sex with another human being. Who we have it with and how we have it has changed, the desire remains the same. It's neither good nor bad; it just is. It's not a judgment – just truth.

Now that you understand more about your sexual energy center, are you ready to send an energetic love message to someone? Are you nervous about meeting someone? Learn how to send an energetic love letter and you will begin to communicate comfortably.

CHAPTER TEN

Sending Energetic Love Letters

C an show you love somebody by accepting them for who they are? Can you allow someone to be just where they are? When you live in the moment and trust yourself enough to be in each and every moment, you always attract who and what is appropriate for you.

In this chapter, learn how you can send appreciation and affection to someone. When you send an energetic message to someone without any expectations on how it must be, you create room for love and affection to return to you.

What is the Glue for Any Relationship?

YOU MAY BE thinking sex. Or, communication. Trust is the glue for any relationship. Trust, let go, and be yourself. Can you trust yourself? Or others? In what ways are you limited to trusting yourself or others?

As Bob Dylan's song says,

> *"Trust yourself. And you won't be disappointed when vain people let you down. Trust yourself. And look not for answers where no answers can be found. Don't trust me to show you love. When my love may be only lust. If you want somebody you can trust, trust yourself."*

93

When you don't trust yourself, you don't trust others. If you don't trust yourself, it shows up in others. In other words, you attract people and situations that you cannot trust.

Confidence and inner trust are one and the same in the emotional state. Confidence is your ability to cope and depend upon yourself to create a reality that is dependable. If you don't have confidence, you will create a reality that you cannot depend upon.

Self Love and Trust Create Miracles

TRUST IS A unity factor. It unites your whole being and causes miracles to happen. Instead of searching for trust and acceptance from others, tell yourself you already have it, then use it, become it.

> ## Self Love TIP # 17
>
> **Treat yourself with kindness, others will reciprocate.**

When you trust yourself, you navigate challenging emotions such as grief, anger, or fear. Accept with your heart and soul that you are loved, even if you're not sure who, when, where, how, you will attract it. Without effort, you attract more of what you are into your life.

Do Something Special for Yourself

STOP JUDGING YOURSELF. You are valuable. You have the power to do something special for yourself. What will it be? Start by accepting every choice, thought, emotion, action. Let's say you regret criticizing your friend. Maybe you've held onto a grudge far too long. When you value your personal abilities and what they can give to you, you show yourself love.

Francine was hard on herself at a workshop. She became aware about how her 'lusting' emotions and seductive behavior attracted previous lovers. The more she judged herself, the more she withdrew from people around her. This created more separation between her and her desire for a loving relationship.

With my guidance, she practiced accepting herself a little each day and worked with the visualizations in this book. She began to notice others around her respond favorably, inviting her to social events and other activities she never considered doing before.

> "Trust yourself. Create the kind of self that you will be happy to live with all your life"
>
> Golda Meir

How Do You Show Your Love to Others?

AS YOU LEARN to control your sexual and emotional energy center, you gain confidence in your self. You increase your ability to trust yourself and love others. Your natural attractiveness begins to radiate inner confidence and self love to the world.

Do you show love to others like you want them to love you? Or do you have unrealistic expectations about how others should treat you? What energetic messages are you sending out to your relationships?

Projecting Your Expectations for Love

IF YOUR LOVE is based on 'projection', it won't last. Do you impose your own perceptions and expectations onto another person? When you impose or project expectations on someone, you are in love with a fantasized image, not a real person. Highly deceptive, this can create enormous disappointment.

"Love is always bestowed as a gift - freely, willingly, and without expectation.... We don't love to be loved; we love to love."

Leo Buscaglia

Loving the "Wrong" Person

ARE YOU IN a relationship with someone who cannot love you back? Are you with someone who does not treat you well or provide a compatible partnership? Unconsciously, you are attracting this experience to yourself. Maybe you modeled your parents' behaviors. On an unconscious level, you have set a pattern of choosing wrong partners. Your energy is attracting to you what is familiar to you on some level. The familiar, even though not fully satisfying, is more comfortable than the unknown.

> **Self Love Tip # 18**
>
> **To break a pattern of attracting the same type of relationship, become aware of it.**

Karen found herself giving up all the things she wanted in her relationship to make her partner happy. She became bored and eventually resented her relationship. She started having multiple love affairs that also soon became unfulfilling. She realized her sex partners zapped her energy leaving her emotionally flat. Karen was frustrated that she wasn't receiving the love she deserved.

She attracted the opposite sex easily, and thought that was all it took. After consulting me, she realized she was attracting unsatisfying relationships. Sex wasn't her answer, but loving herself was. When she committed herself to loving herself, her current relationship improved and she no longer felt the need for extra sexual activity outside it.

Loving Spiritual Agreements

SOMETIMES, EVEN WHEN you are expressing who and what you think you are, you may attract someone you feel has a lot to learn. On a spiritual level, you make all kinds of agreements to be of service to others. Sometimes you make agreements to be an example for others to help them find their own strengths and abilities.

Ponder This

You cannot be in any relationship unless your spiritual agreement is co-creation and having similar vibrations. You attract exactly who is supposed to be with you, in that moment. You are on a spiritual journey of learning about love, being love, giving and receiving love.

Do You Feel Safe to Love?

ARE YOU IN a relationship that will not allow you to be your real self? Are you in a relationship that is not satisfying, but you stay in it because you feel safe? Maybe you are not safe with the idea of taking full responsibility for who and what you are? Or who and what you could be?

If you feel you need to keep yourself safe or protected, you will end up limiting the type of relationships you create.

Stop Resisting Your Natural Loving Self

WHEN YOU STOP resisting your natural loving self, your reality will automatically change. Loving and supportive relationships will come into your life. Would you rather be alone than express your true inner needs?

If you are in a relationship where you do not feel safe or comfortable expressing your deepest inner needs, you are alone anyway. You are simply alone together.

To Create Relationships with Love and Joy

IN CREATING RELATIONSHIPS that work with love and joy, it is important to express your vulnerability. This really means you are open to all that you are. Being vulnerable is a strength, not a weakness. It is full and total trust.

Vulnerability does not mean being open to everyone and everything so they can take pot shots at you. It means being open and available to your true self. When you open up to yourself, you are open and available to the infinite Source of all creation. Connecting to your infinite creation will bring you love, peace, confidence and power. It makes your life real, joyful and magical.

> *"There is more hunger for love and appreciation in this world than for bread."*
>
> Mother Teresa

www.amirahhall.com © 2015
LOVE UP Your Life

amirah@amirahhall.com

Unspoken Loving Communication

MOST OF THE problems that occur in relationships are caused by what is not being said, rather than what is said. Non communication, or withheld communication, is simply another way you hold back the real you from your partner. The problem with unspoken communication is more complex than might first be perceived. Saying "everything is all right," when you are thinking "drop dead," won't fool the other person for very long.

The other person intuitively picks up your heart's truth and honest feelings. Count on it! It is the same sense that tells you when there has been a big fight or disagreement as you step into a strangely quiet and tense room.

It is the same sense that you use intuitively to energetically scan large groups of strangers at a party, as you decide who would be interesting to spend an evening getting to know.

The Power of Direct Unspoken Communication

AN ACQUAINTANCE OF mine who is well versed in martial arts, uses direct unspoken communication by intent. He uses it to defeat powerful and well known karate masters. Gifted in his own right, this particular man is very aware of the power of unspoken communication. He uses it to his advantage when he takes his preliminary bows as his match begins. He smiles on the outside while mentally projecting extreme violence towards his opponent.

His opponent energetically and mentally picks up these projected waves of discordant energy. These waves temporarily short out his opponents' power centers, making it almost impossible for them to defend themselves as the bout begins.

Flourishing Loving Relationships

IN ORDER TO grow and flourish, every relationship requires open and honest communication coming from a point of inner truth and balance. Honest communication enables the other person to truly relate and to have a relationship with who you actually are. Open, clear, conscious communication enables the other person to observe and act with trust. They know where they stand with you and respond favorably.

> **Self Love Tip # 19**
>
> **Be clear and direct in your communication. You won't be sending one message verbally and another mismatched or opposing one psychically. Share what is in your heart with trust, honest, and clarity.**

Be Creative, Trust and Play

FROM A RELAXED state, can you express yourself with trust and creative joy? Do you feel balanced within yourself?

Relationships are created by simply learning how to play with each other. Learn how to love and accept yourself unconditionally; trust who and what you are. When you share yourself in a relationship, you feel your own sense of completeness, and realize you are never alone.

To have a successful relationship, you must awaken the divine young child inside yourself first. A young child is full of curiosity and knows the universe is beautiful and full of surprises. A young child naturally loves and trusts in a positive way. A young child is naturally truthful and lives within integrity. A young child is more occupied with being natural, not normal. A young child lets their imagination soar, unlimited in the creation of a magical and miraculous world. Always, always seek out a good playmate for your primary relationships, and especially someone who knows how to play fair.

Allow yourself to remember this world is magical, and allow that magic and enchantment back into your life. Be who you are, and do the things you love to do as often as you can! That is really the only way to really live your life.

Sending Positive Love Letter

WHETHER YOU REALIZE it or not, you automatically visualize everything you want. When you send conscious positive feelings of attraction to a person they can respond spontaneously without the need for words. The purpose of sending an energetic love letter is not to control another person or impose your energy on them. You simply unlock loving feelings much faster than trying to find the right words and dealing with uneasy conversations.

www.amirahhall.com © 2015
LOVE UP Your Life

amirah@amirahhall.com

On a first date for example, it will allow you to enjoy another person's company and watch the relationship unfold naturally. In an established relationship, it will allow you to move beyond words and have more fun faster.

Send an Energetic Love Letter Visualization

HAVE YOU EVER wanted to energetically send someone a message that you were attracted to them? Sending an Energetic Love Letter is special because it will be sent from you with no one in the middle to interfere.

> **Ponder this**
>
> You have free will to send thoughts. Others have free will to respond favorably or rejecting them.

You can send a message to anyone you feel attracted to with the confidence that your good intentions and warm feelings will definitely be received. Some people will respond by sending their own message and others will NOT open the envelope. Either way, you are simply sending your love into the world. Everyone has some form of intuition and will pick up these thoughts.

1. To send an energetic love letter look at your special someone in the eyes. You can do this in person or in thought.

2. Imagine sending them affection, love through the air.

3. Envision thoughts of fondness and warmth going to them.

4. Imagine you are sending your love and affection in the air toward the person.

5. Imagine your affection going to their soul.

LISTEN to Guided Meditation http://amirahhall.com/images/audio/ loveupyourlife.mp3

"We are all born for love...it is the principle existence and it's only end."

Disraeli

Final Words About This Book

PEOPLE SENSE WHEN you are carrying obstructions in your energy field and sense when it is clear. As you clear your thoughts, emotions and old programs, you begin to radiate your true nature – LOVE. You then effortlessly, attract more of what you are – LOVE. Are you ready to optimize your life force energy?

Commitment to practice this book's visualizations for 20-30 days will give you optimum results. It might take you up to six months but with practice the visualizations in this book are effective and powerful tools at to assist you in having a more vibrant sex appeal. You have everything within you to LOVE UP Your Life.

About the Author

*a*mirah Hall is an international quantum energy mentor and speaker. Her personal story is inspiring with over 30 years of inner discovery and overcoming life-threatening obstacles. Amirah uses her life experiences including a near-death experience for the benefit of others guiding others through personal issues that continue block and weigh them down.

In her work as an expert clairvoyant energy healer, Amirah shares hidden secrets of regeneration and renewal using quantum activation techniques and guided meditation. Her masterful transformational skills provide an integrated, fast track for manifesting, maintaining and growing abundant health, wealth and inner joy.

After a NDE in 1998 Amirah's life transformed as she underwent a spiritual struggle integrating her extra-ordinary abilities into the physical world. She left behind a successful career in corporate sales for following her passion for healing herself and others.

Amirah consulted Royal Family Members in Dubai and many thousands of individuals worldwide. She has been a featured expert on Dubai One TV, NBC 7, San Diego Business Journal, Dubai Universities and the Ritz Carlton. She is a featured writer for publications including Dubai's Gulf News, San Diego's The Light Connection. Amirah is the author of WAKE UP Shift Happens, and co-author of #1 Amazon Best Selling book, Transforming through 2012 and Beyond.

Combining her healing abilities, quantum awareness, and life experience, Amirah can help you dissolve energetic barriers preventing your wellbeing, abundance, love and harmonious relationships with self and others. Every session with Amirah is directed by the individual's needs with their divine blueprint. Private consultations: http://www.amirahhall.com/homepage/transformation.html.

Kind Words from Others

"Amirah, M.Msc. is an intuitive coach extraordinaire. She is the next Sylvia Browne."

Paige, Edmond, WA

"I have practiced the Visualization only a few times and people are already responding differently to me. It's as if I am no longer invisible."

David, Cincinnati, OH

"The techniques Amirah teaches have been practical and miraculous in my life. She is extremely gifted and I removed blocks forever. Changes are taking place in my life and my friends notice it too. Amirah's ability to see the 'unseen' is truly amazing".

Laura, San Diego, CA

"I think Amirah is the most powerful intuitive I have encountered. She accurately imparted information to me. Amirah is certainly sharing her ability with the world. What a gift to experience her work. I highly recommend her classes and readings."

Tamara, San Diego, CA

"Since my consultation with Amirah, I am more in tune with my body and surroundings. I feel more alive and awake."

Marie, Chula Vista, CA

"The tools Amirah teaches in her class have allowed me to tap into a higher consciousness, which has yielded tangible benefits in my life, both on a personal and professional level".

Henry, Spring Valley, CA

"My soul feels cleaner and I feel much clearer about my path in life."

Brooke, Denver, CO

"I have experienced major life improvements and Amirah helped me to identify underlying blocks in my life."

John, Scottsdale, AZ

"Amirah cleared my house's energy - it sold in record time for our asking price with all the contingency plans approved. This was amazing since our house was listed for over a year ago with no results and five other homes were for sale on our block."

Kathy, Truckee, CA

"I am less fearful and feel capable and strong. I feel there is light at the end of the tunnel."

Dori, Escondido, CA

"Amirah's support has been key to me during a difficult life transition. I don't know what I would have done without her. I certainly don't think my life would be turning out this good and really changing so easily. So much love to you, along with my very deep gratitude and respect."

Deborah, New York, NY

"Amirah has a wonderful way of presenting material with humor that really works. Her consultation and classes have eased my stress. I could literally feel the entire class responding positively, which is a tribute to her user-friendly approach coupled with your strong abilities in this area. Amirah has a valuable service to offer, and presents it in a way that is down-to-earth and understandable.

Tom, Los Angeles, CA

www.amirahhall.com © 2015
LOVE UP Your Life

amirah@amirahhall.com

Made in the USA
Monee, IL
01 April 2022